Sunset
Landscaping for Privacy

By the Editors of Sunset Books
and Sunset Magazine

Lane Publishing Co. • Menlo Park, California

Produced and Designed by The Compage Company
In cooperation with the Editors of Sunset

Editor
Kenneth R. Burke

Text
Rex Wolf

Associate Editor
Jessie Wood

Graphic Design
Williams and Ziller Design

Photographer
Michael McKinley

Additional Photography
Derek Fell: Page 6 bottom, 53 top, 75 top right,
77 bottom, 83 top right, 92 bottom
Pamela Harper: Page 6 top, 12, 13, 29 top, 37, 44 top,
62, 67 bottom right, 77 top, 86, 93 bottom

Back cover photograph by Michael McKinley

Illustrations
Rik Olson

Consultants
Alvin Horton
A. Cort Sinnes

Typesetting
Terry Robinson & Co.

Cover
Hedge and trees beyond the upper terrace shield
this colorful, intimate outdoor living area from a busy street
and neighboring houses. Photograph by Glenn Christiansen.

Editor, Sunset Books: David E. Clark

C O N T E N T S

OUTDOOR LIVING SPACES

Privacy is important to the quality of life. Everybody needs a certain amount of privacy, to relax and enjoy time alone or with family or friends. A little seclusion, a safe retreat from the world, makes it easier to cope with the pressures of life.

Your garden can be such a retreat. Gaining privacy in your yard doesn't mean that you have to give your neighbors the cold shoulder. You can provide a buffer between you and your neighbors that they will enjoy as much as you will.

The primary emphasis in this book is on creating privacy for you and your household, away from the intrusions of the outside world. But the concept of privacy can also be expanded to include protection from having to view unattractive things—a laundry area, a potting shed, or a telephone pole bristling with wires. Anything that detracts from your enjoyment of and sense of security in your garden is a candidate for concealment by plantings or structures.

Just as your home is composed of a number of rooms arranged in a convenient manner to serve the different aspects of your life, so can the property around your home be a series of outdoor spaces that will complement and enhance your lifestyle. These garden "rooms" can be natural extensions of various interior rooms, or they can be independent and discrete from the house. Just as walls, doors, dividers, and curtains in various configurations are used to create spaces within a house, so walls, fences and gates, pergolas, hedges, trees, and vines are used to create private spaces in the garden.

There may be areas around your home that you don't use because of lack of privacy. This book will help you take a hard look at all your outdoor areas to see if you can create a living space where none now exists, or improve the usability of existing outdoor areas. Although many of the examples in this book are based on a house on a fairly large suburban lot, the principles and methods of creating privacy are equally applicable to almost any type of home and garden. Whether you must work within the constraints of a small urban lot, live in an apartment with just a balcony garden, or are faced with restrictions in a townhouse development, this book will give you the information you need to create attractive, functional private spaces out of public or unused ones.

Left: Banks of ivy and juniper enclose an entry court. Swags of Lady Banks roses growing in an oak tree provide a curtain of flowers during the summer. Design: Thomas Church, San Francisco, CA. **Right:** This small back garden invites you to kick off your shoes and relax after a day's work. A sunken fountain contributes its soothing sound to the atmosphere. Design: David Poot, Seattle, WA.

A FLOWERING SCREEN

The small paved sitting area above is enclosed by tall-growing and brightly blooming perennials. Design: Mrs. Muriel Mullings.

PRIVACY AND SHADE

This pleasant sitting area off a studio, shown at left with the sketch below, is covered by a grape arbor, which provides shade during the summer but lets the winter sun shine through. Design: Innocenti and Webel, Old Brookville, NY.

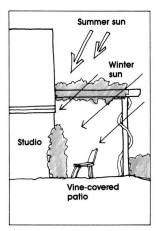

PRIVATE SPACES TO SUIT YOUR LIFESTYLE

In evaluating the potential of outdoor areas, it helps to have a clear idea of the uses to which you will put your private spaces. Examine your lifestyle. What activities around the house do you enjoy now, and which would you enjoy more, or more often, if you had more private space? A vegetable garden, or sunbathing, or barbecuing for large numbers of friends all have differing requirements for space and privacy.

Here's a short checklist of various ways you may enjoy using your property:

■ *Entertaining*. Do you like to entertain frequently? Large groups of people, or small groups of two or three couples?

■ *Recreation*. Basketball court, lawn for badminton or croquet, a full-size swimming pool—each requires something different in terms of space and privacy.

■ *Relaxation*. Do you want a sunny spot for sunbathing or a shady spot to curl up with a good book? How about a hot tub or spa? Its placement may be determined by the amount of privacy you can achieve.

■ *Gardening*. If you like to create spectacular displays of plants for all to admire, then by all means create a front garden to turn the heads of passersby. If, however, you wish to create a more intimate garden, or conceal the utility shed, then you'll need to provide some sort of barrier or shelter. Also be sure to take into account how much time you'll want to spend maintaining the garden.

TAKING STOCK

Once you've got a good idea what kind of outdoor living spaces you could use, it's time to take inventory of what you have to work with. Even if you're remodeling a landscape you've lived with for years, a close look at its advantages and disadvantages—a "re-viewing"—will be useful. Creating an annotated map of your property will help you to be more objective about what you've got to work with. Your plan doesn't have to be elaborate; but in the long run, the more information you include the better off you'll be. Walk all the way around the perimeter of your lot, probe into every corner, and survey your views from every angle. A complete review of your property helps dispel preconceived and ill-considered notions. You may conclude that the brick sitting area you have in mind is best suited to the back of your lot, where it will be sheltered by the garage, and that the patch of crabgrass in the front should be transformed into a low-maintenance sweep of juniper.

When you make up your plan, you will probably want to include the following information:

■ *Boundary lines*. It may sound obvious, but if you're contemplating any construction, or planning to plant trees and shrubs along a boundary, you'd better make absolutely sure that the boundary between you and a neighbor is in fact where you think it is. If it later proves to be incorrect and your construction or planting turns out to be on neighboring property, your neighbor can compel you to move it or tear it down. If you're at all unsure about your boundaries, invest in the insurance of having your property surveyed. Draw your boundaries to scale; ⅛ inch to 1 foot is a convenient scale.

■ *Position of the house*. Draw the outline of the house and any other structures (such as a garage or tool shed) to scale in their correct positions. Also indicate the rooms of the house. This will help you identify possible locations for outdoor rooms that could be extensions of interior rooms.

■ *Existing plantings*. Sketch the locations and give descriptions of *all* the existing plants you want to keep. Sometimes it's easy to forget about tall trees that are so familiar that they become a seemingly immutable part of the landscape.

Think twice before you decide to eliminate large plants or groupings of plants. If you've always hated that pyracantha, by all means take it out; but be sure that it won't leave a gaping hole in your landscape that you'll later wish were plugged with something.

THE BASE PLAN

Making a base plan will show you what you have to work with—and against. This plan shows the boundary lines of the property, the position of the house and swimming pool, the direction of prevailing winds, and views into the yard from neighboring structures. This plan is for a newly built house with no existing plantings; if you are remodeling an existing garden, you should include in your plan all established plantings that you wish to keep.

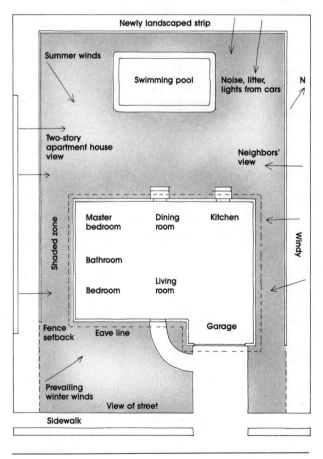

Winter: 9 hours of daylight. Sun low in southern sky, long shadows to north.

Spring and Fall: 12 hours of daylight. Sun higher in southern sky, still some shadows to north.

Summer: 15 hours of daylight. Sun almost directly overhead, few shadows to north.

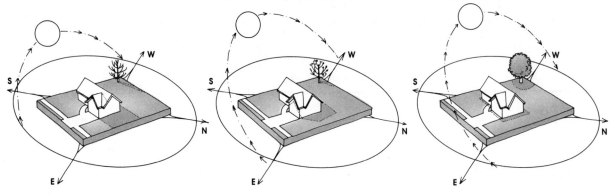

■ *Exposure and wind.* Mark the direction of north on your plan. Remember that the position of the sun changes in the sky with the seasons. The sun is highest in the sky at the start of summer and lowest in the southern sky at the beginning of winter. Mark the areas that receive summer sun and winter sun.

Indicate the direction of regular winds and the time of year if they vary by season, and note any areas of wind turbulence caused by structures. You'll want to avoid choosing windy spots for outdoor living areas.

Remember that cold air flows downhill like water, "puddles" in basins, and can be dammed by solid walls and fences. Indicate any slope on your plan to help you avoid creating "frost dams."

SIGHT LINES AND SOUND LINES

In order to determine your privacy needs, you'll have to analyze what you need privacy *from.* A neighbor's second-story window? The house in back, up the hill? The noise from the community swim center next door? Once you've figured from which directions you'll need privacy, you can combine this information with your ideas on which parts of your yard you'll use for what, to come up with where you'll need barriers for what purpose.

Avoid the temptation to make the design process more complicated than it really is. Perhaps all you need is a 6-foot fence around the perimeter of your lot. If your privacy problems are more acute, you can still come up with interesting solutions by following these steps.

1. On your plan, indicate roughly those areas where you would like privacy and what sorts of things would be happening there. If you like to quantify values, you might make up a privacy index and rate the "amount" or importance of privacy within each area. For instance, if you like to soak in your hot tub you'd probably give this area a 10 rating, while the vegetable garden might rate only a 2.

2. Mark on your plan the directions from which others can see into your house and garden and the approximate portions that are open to view. It's sometimes difficult to gauge exactly how much other people can see if access is limited. You'll be able to check out what pedestrians can see from the street; and if you're well acquainted with your neighbors, you can explore their views.

Keep in mind that even though it may be *possible* for a neighbor to look into your yard, it may not be *probable.* Concentrate on creating privacy in only your most open areas, or those to which you've given a high privacy rating.

3. Browse through this book to collect ideas for natural and constructed barriers that you can employ to ensure your privacy. Remember that it's not always necessary to have *absolute* privacy; sometimes all you need is a buffer that gives you a sense of being sheltered from the outside world.

This is where the privacy ratings mentioned above can be helpful. If you have an area with a top privacy rating of 10, for example, you would probably decide to limit your options to solid walls or fences. For a dining area rated 6 or 7, a low fence and trellis or a couple of lath screens might suffice.

Once again, keep in mind the mature size and effect of the trees or shrubs you plant, and how structures will appear to your neighbors. A fast-growing coast redwood may very well block the view down from your neighbor's master bedroom on your patio, but it might also completely block *any* view from that window. Both you and your neighbors may enjoy the brilliant yellow flowers and soft gray foliage of a hedge of *Acacia baileyana,* but if it's adjacent to their swimming pool, they won't appreciate all the seed pods they have to fish out every summer.

PUTTING IT ALL TOGETHER

Now you need to match your list of desired uses with your map of desirable locations. That's the essence of it, although of course in practice landscape design is a lot more complicated than that. This book offers some observations and suggestions that may be helpful to your planning. For a short course in landscape design, see the Sunset book *Landscaping Illustrated.*

Even if local ordinances don't require it, it's a good idea to design *low* streetside fences or hedges near driveways, to give drivers an unimpeded view of pedestrian and vehicular traffic.

FEELING OVERWHELMED?

If your budget permits, you can turn the nitty-gritty design details, building, and planting over to a landscape architect or landscape contractor. Even if you plan to do most of the design, construction, and planting work yourself, you may want to call in a landscaping professional to evaluate or polish your final plans. An advisor can help you to prevent costly mistakes as well as inject new ideas into your plans.

Whenever you consult a professional, you'll get the best results by specifying precisely what you want and expect. Formulate a budget so your advisor knows how much you can afford to spend. Professional help need not be extremely costly, especially if you consult a landscape architect or landscape designer on a limited basis. The advice or suggestions you receive will probably be well worth the cost. Ask your friends and neighbors to recommend professionals with whom they have worked.

LOCAL ORDINANCES

Many communities have ordinances governing the height and placement of constructed barriers such as walls and fences. Natural screens, such as shrubs and hedges, are usually less strictly regulated, but some restrictions may still apply. Check with your local planning department or building inspector to find out what your local requirements are.

BEING NICE TO YOUR NEIGHBORS

You can provide for your own privacy without impinging on your neighbors' sight lines or making them feel "walled out." Remember that the 5-foot sapling you plant today could turn into a 50-foot giant in just a few years. Don't plant a tree where it might block a neighbor's view completely; the idea is to deflect views from your private spaces, not to obliterate them totally.

Consider other long-term effects of major plantings on your neighbors. Will the mature height of the tree you're planting plunge your neighbor's swimming pool into shadow in the afternoon? Will the thick hedge you like so much prove invasive and plague your neigh-

bors with its incursions into the adjoining flower bed? When you're considering property-line plantings, remember that the same maintenance chores will be necessary on both sides of the planting; unless you're willing to shoulder all the maintenance, your neighbors may justifiably resent the additional work involved.

Your best bet, of course, is to enlist your neighbor's support and, ideally, participation from the very start of your planning. It may be that a combined effort will provide both of you with privacy so that both are pleased. A joint venture has the additional advantages of shared installation costs and maintenance.

WHAT PRICE PRIVACY?

How much you need to spend to create a private outdoor living space depends on the cost of materials and the cost of labor. Shop around before you decide what materials to use. A concrete block wall will be less expensive than one made of brick. A hedge of English laurel (*Prunus laurocerasus*) will cost even less (although it will be about five years before the plants mature into a full screen). Don't skimp on the quality of your materials, but don't get locked into using expensive materials either; let your imagination roam a bit. Inexpensive materials used boldly can create a more interesting effect than expensive materials used in a boring, run-of-the-mill way.

How much labor you can provide depends on your level of interest, your skills, and your available time. The following chapters contain information on trees, shrubs, and vines that are particularly suitable as living screens. There's not enough space in this book to give step-by-step instructions on how to build a wall or fence, but you will find an overview of the work involved, and references to some excellent books that contain detailed building instructions.

If you don't want to tackle the whole job, consider hiring part of the work done and finishing it yourself. For instance, you could have fence posts and rails installed and finish the relatively simple procedure of nailing on the facing yourself.

MAINTENANCE

If you decide on a privacy screen of living plants, it's useful to estimate, while you're still in the planning stage, how much time and effort you're willing to spend on maintenance. A fast-growing hedge that needs clipping once a month to look its best will take much more maintenance time than a redwood fence that may only need a coat of sealer every couple of years. Or a row of bushy pine trees, which need only an annual light pruning and topping, might be just what your landscape calls for.

CHOOSING PLANTS

Later sections will cover selecting specific trees, shrubs, hedges, and vines to achieve your desired effect. While you're in the planning stage—or even earlier, in the thinking-about-it stage—take the time to tour local nurseries and garden centers looking for plants that appeal to you. If there's a botanical or other public garden nearby, check out the kinds of landscapes displayed there.

Here are a few generalities to keep in mind while you're choosing your plants for privacy.

Fast versus slow growers. This is always a tricky decision. Fast-growing plants will give a mature look and screening in a relatively short period. On the other hand, fast-growing plants require much more maintenance to keep them trimmed, and most are relatively short-lived.

Steering a middle course is usually the wisest decision. Include in your landscape a combination of fast and slow-growing plants. Plant as generously as your budget can afford. This will give your new landscape a lush effect, and the plants can be thinned as they grow and need more room. Bear in mind, however, that fast-growing plants compete for water, nutrients, sunlight, and space, and can seriously inhibit or even cripple their slower-growing neighbors if not kept in check. You might also consider a screen of lath or canvas that can be dismantled after your plants have reached their desired height.

Deciduous versus evergreen. Plants that lose all their leaves in the autumn and gain a new set in the spring are called *deciduous*. Plants that shed a few leaves or needles throughout the year, but maintain most of their leaves or needles at all times, are called *evergreen*. Healthy evergreens will provide a green screen all year long, while deciduous plants have bare branches during winter. The lack of winter leaves on deciduous trees is often an advantage, as it lets more light through during the darker winter months. Or perhaps the area screened by a deciduous plant isn't used during the winter, so privacy isn't needed then. Many deciduous trees have the added attribute of spring or summer blossoms, or brilliant fall foliage, to add visual interest to your garden all year round.

Annuals and perennials. Annuals and perennials are nonwoody bedding plants. As their name suggests, annuals have a life cycle of one year. Perennials live for many years, but most die back each winter and reappear the following spring.

You'll probably want to depend on more substantial plants for most of your privacy screens, but both annuals and perennials include many species that are fast growing and can serve as temporary summertime screens.

Foliage color and texture. As you're picking out plants you like and pencilling them in on your plan, keep in mind each plant's foliage color and texture and how those qualities relate to the plants around them.

Leaves aren't just green, they're light green, dark green, shiny green, or gray green. Many species of plants have different varieties that closely resemble each other except for certain characteristics such as foliage color, mature size, or flower color. Plant hybridizers often introduce varieties with variegated foliage—multicolored leaves that have touches of red, white, or yellow. The texture of the foliage depends on many factors: the size of the leaves and how they are arranged on their stems, the shape of the leaves, the edges of the leaves, and their profusion.

You can either contrast two radically different foliages or pick foliages that are somewhat similar and that will blend together well. Use contrasting foliages with restraint; although dissimilar combinations can add interest and emphasis to a landscape, too many contrasts makes for a choppy effect. A similarity in foliage will lend a sense of unity to your landscape design.

Climate zones. Few plants can take the heat of the southern summer and be equally happy during a northern winter. When specific plants are recommended in this book, you will also find information about which zones in the United States and Canada are best for that plant.

The plant hardiness map on the opposite page has been adapted from the climate zones developed by the United States Department of Agriculture, and is used by many garden catalogs and books. Zones are based on average expected low winter temperatures. Use the map to locate the hardiness zone in which you live.

The limitations of a map of this scale are apparent. You may be on the borderline between two zones where the zone assignment could go either way. The simplification inherent in a hardiness map does not acknowledge other significant factors in climate that affect plant growth, such as humidity, expected high temperatures, and wind. A zone map based only on minimum expected temperatures cannot account for variations in microclimates within each zone, not to mention within a single garden.

Within a garden, for example, a south-facing wall may hold enough warmth to carry an otherwise tender plant through the winter. Spreading evergreen trees provide a measure of winter protection to plants beneath them. Conversely, a wall or fence across a slope can trap cold air, producing an area that is colder than the rest of the garden.

If you live in an area not shown on the map, obtain the average temperature from local sources. Then find the zone in which your average temperature falls.

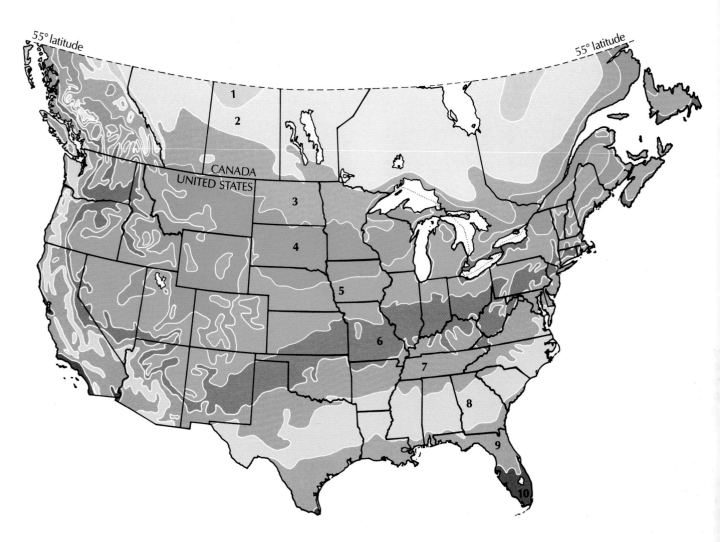

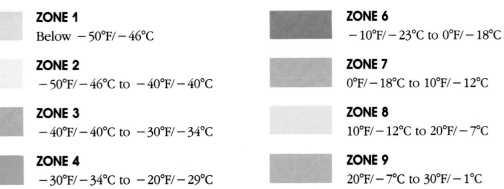

ZONE 1
Below −50°F/−46°C

ZONE 2
−50°F/−46°C to −40°F/−40°C

ZONE 3
−40°F/−40°C to −30°F/−34°C

ZONE 4
−30°F/−34°C to −20°F/−29°C

ZONE 5
−20°F/−29°C to −10°F/−23°C

ZONE 6
−10°F/−23°C to 0°F/−18°C

ZONE 7
0°F/−18°C to 10°F/−12°C

ZONE 8
10°F/−12°C to 20°F/−7°C

ZONE 9
20°F/−7°C to 30°F/−1°C

ZONE 10
30°F/−1°C to 40°F/4°C

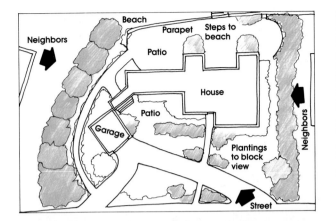

PLANTINGS SCREEN A QUARTER ACRE

The sketch to the left illustrates the arrangement of the James River, VA garden shown in the photographs on this page and opposite. The house is placed across the quarter-acre lot with a loggia at right angles to the left end of the house extending to the end of the garage. This sequence of structures creates the surround for a secluded front patio that is shielded from the street by shrubs and small trees. Pathways wind along the sides of the house, which are protected from neighbors by evergreen shrubs and trees. The back of the house gives onto a broad brick terrace that overlooks the sea.

Opposite page. Top left: This view from the street shows how lines of sight are broken up by trees and shrubs. *Top right:* The path from the driveway near the garage toward the front patio. *Center:* The front patio, looking from the loggia toward the front door. *Bottom left:* The front walk, leading to the main entrance. *Bottom right:* Looking into the loggia from the front patio. *This page. Above:* The miniature rose 'Pillow Talk' on the back terrace is one of many container plants that provide spots of color on the paved areas. *Left:* The view toward the other end of the back terrace. The planting beds along the perimeter protect children (and adults) from the steep drop-off below the terrace.

BETWEEN YOU AND THE STREET

If you take a long hard look at the space available on your property with an eye to setting up a private garden, you may be surprised at what you discover. Have you considered your front yard as a prime site for creating a secluded bit of garden and sitting area? Many homeowners have transformed such seldom-used areas in front of their houses into private retreats.

Besides creating additional outdoor living space, you may be able to enhance the graciousness of your entry path and main entry. Streetside protective landscaping can also increase the privacy of the street-facing rooms of the house.

How you landscape the area between the street and your house is up to you—as long as you take into account your neighbors' feelings and the strictures of local building ordinances. This is a somewhat ambiguous space in our society, privately owned, but traditionally treated as public in character. Its development is controlled by local restrictions and by social expectation.

Many developers and homeowners treat the space between house front and street like the old-fashioned parlor—a place to show off to guests but seldom to be enjoyed by the family. The usual landscape approach is to cover most of the area with lawn and then embellish it with a few nonfunctional shrubs and trees. This high-maintenance garden parlor may account for a sizable portion of your lot.

The open, unobstructed approach to front-garden landscaping is fostered by local codes and seems deeply rooted in American culture. This sociable interest in what's going on up and down the street may derive from an earlier period of house design and street layout when the living room faced the street and the front porch was an important place for neighbors to sit and visit. The grander houses were set farther back; their vast lawns and shrubbery borders were symbols of wealth and status. Even modest houses were placed on larger lots than are customary today, so that space itself provided a barrier of sorts.

A FRONT YARD PLAN

The basic plan has been amended to show a possible landscaping arrangement of the front yard. A fence with a gate has been built to the right of the driveway, blocking the view into the right side yard and the back yard. A screen—which could be small trees, a hedge, a fence, or a masonry wall—protects the outdoor sitting and eating area from view. A low hedge along the left boundary defines that limit of the property.

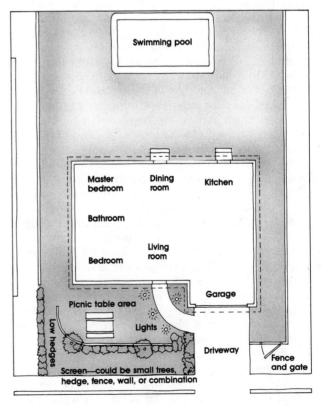

Swimming pool

Master bedroom | Dining room | Kitchen

Bathroom

Bedroom | Living room

Garage

Picnic table area

Low hedges

Lights

Driveway

Fence and gate

Screen—could be small trees, hedge, fence, wall, or combination

Opposite: A classically inspired urban courtyard has been reclaimed from a little-used front lawn. This view is from a second-story window; access to the totally private courtyard is through French doors from the living room. The fence is shingled to match the house. Design: David Poot, Seattle, WA.

In any neighborhood, not every house can have the ideal orientation; the warmest sun or the coolest shade may be on the street side of the house. Spreading out on the front lawn to picnic or sunbathe without some kind of screening seems inappropriate to many people. Still, it's possible to reclaim that "parlor" as usable outdoor living space. With a little taste and imagination, you can create space that is no longer wide open to the street and to passersby. If necessary, you can include a "public" area just large enough to blend with others along the street, while reserving most of the space for your private use and enjoyment.

PLANNING CONSIDERATIONS

Let's explore some of the considerations you should review before you decide to plant a hedge or build a wall. Factors that will influence your planning of your front yard landscape include:

■ The size of the yard and its exposure
■ The uses to which it will be put
■ Local building ordinances
■ The amount of noise you have to contend with and the frequency and intensity of the traffic on your street
■ Security considerations

SIZE AND EXPOSURE

With an open mind, take the time to get to know your front yard intimately. Walk slowly over every square foot of it, pausing frequently to gaze in all directions, scouting for pleasing views or secluded spots. Just because there's a flower bed next to the front door now doesn't mean there can't be a patio there in the future. Be bold and investigate every possibility, no matter how unlikely.

You'll probably want to keep most trees and favorite shrubs, but make a determined effort to clear your mind of all preconceptions of what the front yard *should* look like. The entry path doesn't have to be an offshoot of the driveway. A slope could be leveled or terraced. Look for areas that are "right out in the open" around which barriers can be grown or built.

Keep a record of what time of day and of the year the sun hits your front yard and when it's in the shade. The amount of sun received in various areas will also dictate to some extent your choice of plants.

Next, play the pedestrian, surveying your home on foot from various vantage points. Approach the house on the same side of the street going one direction, then the other, then from across the street, both coming and going. Try to observe your front yard the way an average passerby might: basically disinterested, but willing to be distracted.

As you examine your home from the street, take special note of any sites you have previously identified as potential private places. If you're lucky, the view from the street can be modified with only a couple of judicious plantings. Or you may find that a complete surround is necessary.

The size of your front yard will also determine the kind of protection from the street you will need. If your home is set back 50 feet from the sidewalk, you'll

BARRIER HEIGHTS

6-foot fence

Above: Fences need to be at least slightly higher than eye level to provide privacy and not simply separate space.
Below: The optimum height of shrubs and hedges depends on use. Lower heights are best suited for directing pedestrian traffic, taller forms give a sense of enclosure for privacy.

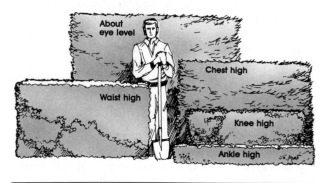

About eye level
Chest high
Waist high
Knee high
Ankle high

need less protection than someone who has an 8-foot strip along the front of the house. Remember that you may need only to break up the view from the street, not to block it off completely.

WHAT WILL YOU USE IT FOR?

The use to which you'll put your new living area out front will determine how much privacy you need and what kind of barriers will be necessary to create that privacy. A cozy spot to sit and read on a sunny winter day will require different protection than a site for a hot tub.

Don't forget that the relationship of the house to the garden may change. When the outdoors becomes more private, you may be able to open up the house to the garden.

CHECK OUT YOUR LOCAL ORDINANCES

Most communities have local codes governing fences and walls in a certain area at the front of the lot, called a *setback*. Restrictions on structures in the setback may vary from a maximum height of 3 feet to a maximum of 6 feet. If you can position your barrier in the area behind the setback, you may be able to avoid any problems with your local planning department or building inspector.

Although local codes governing plantings are often less stringent, trees and shrubs may also be covered by height restrictions, particularly on corner lots where their growth may pose a traffic hazard. Check with your local planning department before you proceed too far in your planning.

TRAFFIC

If you live on a busy street, you'll need to gather information about automobile traffic patterns in order to plan intelligently. What are your objections to the traffic? Is it too noisy? Are exhaust fumes annoying? Is your yard visually exposed to passing traffic? Do headlights sweep across your bedroom ceiling? There's a landscaping solution to each one of those problems. A masonry wall is the most effective sound blocker. Trees and shrubs can help filter polluted air. A lightweight fence or screen covered by a vine can attractively solve the last two problems.

SECURITY

Along with all the other factors you're considering, you should weigh your security concerns. A sturdy wall or fence can be a tremendous asset in protecting your home from intruders. Remember, though, that the more you screen the view of your home from the street and neighbors, the easier it is for someone to break in undetected. Also, if your plans include construction and plantings that would create pockets of shadow in your front yard, be sure to include sufficient outdoor lighting so that you won't be at a disadvantage on a late-night walk to or from your front door.

PROTECTIVE PLANTINGS

Some plants, because of their sharp thorns or dense growth, make excellent protective barriers to deter intruders. The following list offers a small selection of plants that can be used as protective barriers.
Bamboo
Berberis (Barberry)
Chaenomeles (Flowering quince) Some varieties are thornless.
Crataegus (Hawthorn)
Elaeagnus
Pyracantha (Firethorn) Some varieties are thornless.
Rosa (Rose) Species, shrub roses, or climbers will provide the most formidable barrier.

ENTRYWAYS

The entryway is one of the most important elements in your front yard landscape. Visitors to your home will form their first impression while approaching the front door. Your aim is to create a gracious, appealing route for your guests from the sidewalk to the front door.

THE PATHWAY

The trick here is to strike a fine balance between charm and function. It's not natural to walk for any distance in a straight line. Most paths that are allowed to develop naturally run in long, shallow curves. Walks are most interesting when they provide a variety of experiences along the way.

PLANTING FOR PRIVACY IN THE ENTRYWAY ▬▬▬

Before: The unlandscaped front yard is so lacking in privacy that it is virtually useless as an outdoor living space. The entry path may be functional, but the exposed entryway makes the transition from street to house uninviting. The windows at the front of the house are also completely exposed to the street, and passersby can look directly into the house when the front door is open.

After: After landscaping, the lighted path invites visitors toward the front door, which is visually shielded by the small tree to the right. The curved fence to the left of the walk hides a new outdoor eating area. A planting of shrubs softens the fence, while a strategically placed smaller tree increases its effective height. The area on the street side of the fence is treated as a conventional front lawn.

On the other hand, you don't want your guests to get lost or feel confused about the correct route to the front door. There should be no doubt as to which turnings to take. If there are subsidiary paths off the main pathway, visually subordinate them by making them narrower, or by using an "inferior" paving material. For example, gravel is visually subordinate to brick.

Rough stones or aggregate poured concrete may provide interesting textures and visually appealing contrasts in a pathway, but your first concern should be to usher your visitors safely to your front door. By all means use natural paving stones, but be sure they're smooth enough to provide stable footing for those in high heels. You'll also need to provide adequate light so that using the path at night won't be a treacherous experience.

VISUAL SHELTER

In siting natural and constructed barriers between your house and the street, be sure to include an element that blocks the view from the street directly into the house through the front door. It's a small thing, but extremely important in achieving a sense of enclosure and privacy.

ENTRY GATES

An entry or garden gate, working in harmony with a fence or wall, can make an opening statement about your home. It can be airy and informal, or reserved and elegant. Even a low or open-work gate provides a measure of privacy by defining the edge of the garden, and by heightening the contrast between the public and private spaces.

Your best bet is probably to build a gate in the same style as your front fence or wall. A contrasting material, though, is sometimes more interesting than one that is identical to the barrier, and can give the gate added emphasis and prominence. An archway or pergola can visually link the scale of the wall or fence to that of the house. Smothered in a fragrant flowering vine, an archway can provide a dramatic entrance to the front garden.

The width of your gate may be dictated by an existing fence or wall opening. If you're building both a gate and a fence or wall, however, you can adapt the measurements to your particular needs.

The minimum width for a gate is usually 3 feet, but an extra foot in width creates a more gracious feeling. If you expect to be moving gardening equipment or other bulky items through the entry gate, make it even wider. If you have an extra-wide space, consider a two-part gate. For step-by-step instructions on how to build a gate, refer to Sunset's *Garden & Patio Building Book*.

SITTING AREAS

Front-yard sitting areas can be as elaborate or as simple as you care to make them. A small bench surrounded by tall shrubs may be perfect for summer afternoon daydreaming; or you may prefer a formal brick terrace for Sunday morning brunch. Perhaps a ground-level deck

could be tucked between the house and the garage. Or for an older house, what about an old-fashioned screened-in front porch that lets you sit in comfort and see out, but doesn't allow passersby to see in? Let your site, exposure to sun or wind, the activities you enjoy, the proximity of neighbors, and your budget dictate the design of front yard sitting areas. Although it will sometimes be simplest and most expedient to construct a wall or fence all around the front part of your yard, explore and consider as many options as you can think of. Much more interesting effects can often be achieved with groupings of plants and screens, with no loss of privacy.

RISE ABOVE IT ALL

If your house is above the level of the street, consider building a deck off one of the rooms. A light lattice screen planted with vines in containers will effectively conceal people on the deck from passersby. If a neighbor looks down on your deck, you can add overhead visual protection with canvas shades or more lattice and vines. When you expand your outdoor living space above street level, be sure you aren't looming over other neighbors and ruining their privacy.

You don't gain much protection from street noises by moving up; in fact, you'll probably be even more conscious of any racket.

SINK TO NEW DEPTHS

If your front yard is fairly level, consider making it less so by excavating all or a portion of it to lower the grade level. Arranging the sitting area so that it is a couple of feet lower makes an amazing difference. Fences or hedges to screen the area can be less prominent and still be effective. You can use the excavated dirt to form a mound between you and the street; this will increase visual interest, add to the height of any other barriers you may build or plant, and prove an effective sound screen. Drainage of a sunken area requires careful planning, or you may end up with an unwelcome pond when it rains.

PARTIAL SURROUNDS

As an alternative to building or growing a complete barrier all around the front of your yard, consider a screen, hedge, fence, or wall around just the portion of the yard that you will use as a sitting area. This reinforces the idea of an outdoor "room," and creating a specific enclosure is a less elaborate way of gaining privacy without relandscaping the whole front yard. You can also retain some of your front yard as a "public" area to blend with the rest of the landscapes on your street.

Your new outdoor space could be a curved or two-walled wide-angled hedge that protects a new patio or lawn area. Determine the placement of hedges by reviewing the sightlines from the street and planting only where it is necessary to block a particular view. Or your outdoor room could be similar to an indoor one, such as a gazebo constructed of a wood frame and lath, with an overgrowth of vines.

Diagram labels:
House
Roof extension
Pool
Patio
Garage
Wall
Drive
Street noise and view

A LOW WALL AND SCREEN OF TREES

The entry court and sitting area of this home is protected by groves of liquid-ambar trees and a low brick wall (photo at far left). A simple but secure iron gate limits access to the courtyard (photo below). Design: Lani Berrington and Mario Mathias, Manhattan Beach, CA.

WALLING OUT THE WORLD

Under certain circumstances, you may wish to wall off the outside world completely. Designer Thomas Church created a striking and useful enclosure in the front of this San Francisco house set back only 16 feet from the sidewalk.

The sketch of the front garden is shown at bottom left. The brick wall across the front (photo bottom right) is punctuated on the street side by sycamores trained on a metal framework, and by a wrought iron gate into the entry court. (A photo of the entry court can be found on page 44.)

Plantings in the front court off the living room (photo below) are restrained. Colorful blooming plants in containers, such as pink hydrangeas (against the wall) and orchids (right foreground), are changed seasonally for a continuous display. Permanent plantings are limited to a wisteria vine on the wall between the front and entry courts and two more sycamore trees trained on the metal grid. During the growing season a leafy screen breaks the view of neighbors on an up-slope across the street.

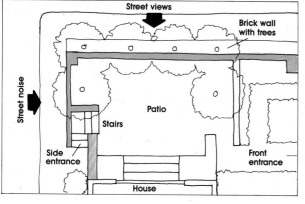

SECLUSION, WITH A GIFT TO THE STREET

As shown in the photos on this page and the sketch at right, a textured and painted brick wall creates a protective enclosure around the front of this house. The view from the street, below, is enlivened by a generous planting of white daisies bordered by purple lobelia and green boxwood. The oversized gate, bottom left, swings outward to invite visitors into the courtyard. Even with the gate open, the sitting area (bottom right) is remarkably secluded and tranquil. Design: David Poot, Seattle, WA.

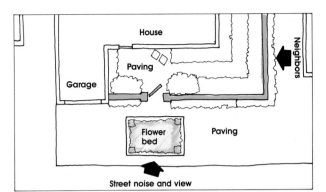

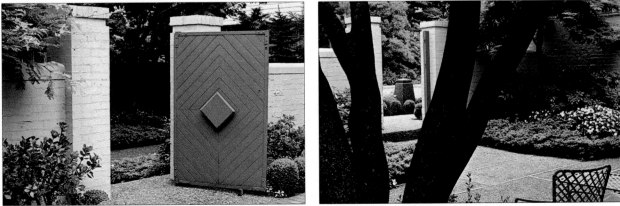

There's no ambiguity about public and private spaces when it comes to back yards. The back yard is traditionally a private space where you can pretty much do what you want, although many communities still restrict the height of any fences, whether in the front yard or back. However, such restrictions shouldn't prevent you from achieving the privacy you desire.

Architects and homebuilders often orient the more open areas of the house toward the back of the lot, recognizing that this is where the occupants feel most relaxed and protected. Therefore the back yard is where you will probably have the greatest freedom to extend the rooms of the house outdoors.

How about an extension of your dining room—a lanai for table and chairs, or benches for outdoor eating? Or an extension of your living room, a place to sit together and chat or entertain friends? Or a charcoal grill as an extension of your kitchen? Or simply a quiet spot for a little well-deserved solitude, a place to get away from it all. Whatever your favorite activities, you can probably find a way to accommodate them in your back yard.

PROVIDING A TRANSITION

As your plans for your back yard landscape develop, keep in mind the transition from house to outdoors. The most fundamental transition from inside to outside is the doorway. To keep costs down, you'll probably want to use existing doorways, but an ambitious project might include repositioning or enlarging the primary access to the back yard.

To soften the transition from house to garden, it is often pleasing to use a structural element that echoes the construction of the house. This may be a purely

Opposite: An inviting, secluded back yard spot. The low-level deck is on the same level as the floor of the house and is built around a mature pine tree whose branches are not visible here. The handsome foliage of *Talauma hodgsonii* shades most of the area. Ceramic inserts in the fence provide a focus for the area. Garden of Lois Brown, Pasadena, CA.

visual device; for instance, a vine-covered trellis built on extensions of the roof rafters combines elements of both house and garden, as well as providing shade and overhead privacy. With a bit of foresight and planning, you can design the transitional elements to be functional as well as esthetically pleasing.

You might want to keep cooking and dining areas close to the house to minimize the length of your back-and-forth trips. More often than not, the primary sitting areas will also be near the house. These transitional areas require some sort of structural element; this could be paving, overhead protection, or a deck. This section explores the advantages of low-level decks as landscaping structures.

LOW-LEVEL DECKS

Don't think of decks as being useful only at great heights or to provide a level area on a sloping lot. Low-level decks are easy to build and offer great flexibility in design, so you can create the transitional space best suited to your needs.

Decks are particularly useful for garden remodeling because they can cover the mistakes of the past. You can use decking for pathways as well as for sitting areas in any part of the yard, which can be a unifying factor if the different decks are all of the same wood or are stained the same color. Decks can be built to almost any shape—rectilinear, curved, free-form—whatever suits your fancy and matches the style of your house and garden.

One of the advantages of designing with decks is that you can vary the height of the deck. A deck at the same level as the floor of the house seems much more an extension of the house than one that drops a couple of feet below the interior. Decks at different levels can help define different areas, such as an entrance deck, a sun-bathing deck, or a dining deck.

Decks make it easy to incorporate large trees or shrubs into your new landscape plan. Solid paving around mature trees and shrubs doesn't allow enough water and nutrients to reach the plants' root systems. Decking lets water and air reach the soil and roots.

A number of different amenities can be built into

This cutaway view of typical deck construction shows how piers, posts, beams, and joists support the decking.

Decking need not always be laid parallel: here are a few of the patterns that can be repeated across your deck.

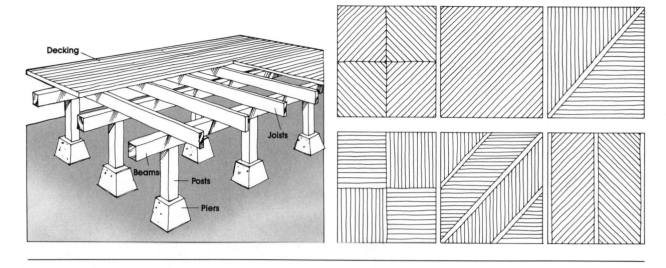

your deck to meet your special needs. A bench around the perimeter can provide lots of seating, act as a guardrail, or double as a display shelf for your favorite container plants. Planter boxes with shrubs or small trees can create a charming nook. Framing for lath screens or uprights for trellises can also be incorporated into your deck design.

Use only decay-resistant wood such as redwood, cypress, cedar heartwood, or pressure-treated lumber. Basic deck construction is shown in the sketch above. You can even buy partly assembled modular deck kits. For a more thorough discussion and complete directions for building decks, refer to the Sunset book *How to Plan & Build Decks.* Maintenance is simple but essential: an annual treatment with a water-repellant wood preservative.

PRIVACY ON YOUR DECK

There are a number of ways to ensure privacy on your deck. As mentioned earlier, you can incorporate built-in planter boxes into your deck design to delineate a private area. Or plant shrubs and small trees in large half-barrels or other portable containers to provide a living screen.

You can, of course, simply fence all or part of the perimeter of your deck. Don't get too massive or solid, though—you don't want the resulting enclosure to be overbearing or claustrophobia-inducing. Perhaps you need only a lath screen 4 or 5 feet high to block the view from the street of people seated on your deck. Trellises and pergolas, overgrown with vines, can block overhead views. They can also provide the framework to hang temporary barriers that can be used only when needed, such as roll-down bamboo or basswood shades or canvas tiebacks. Or try panels of translucent fiberglass that will screen views but allow sunlight to stream through. For your comfort and the health of your plants, design so that air can still circulate.

TAKING STOCK

As you're planning your back yard landscape, you'll find it useful to take inventory of the advantages and disadvantages of your present setup. Also think about the ways you presently use your back yard and what other activities you might enjoy there if you had more privacy. Your conceptualization of the design will be focused and clarified if you draw a plan to rough scale of what you intend to do. Don't be discouraged if it doesn't come together all at once; it takes time to muse and sketch out different possibilities before you come up with a workable plan that will serve your needs.

BACK YARD ACTIVITIES

Make a list of the activities you and the members of your household enjoy in your yard—or would enjoy if your yard were set up for them.

■ *Recreation.* A swimming pool is always a favorite if you have the space, budget, and climate to enjoy it. How about volleyball or croquet on the lawn? If there are children in your family, consider a special play area just for them.

■ *Relaxation.* Hot tubs and spas can be extraordinarily comforting after an arduous day at work. Or you might want a sheltered spot to maintain your tan during the summer. If you're a bookworm or like naps, a shady, cool spot in summer and a protected one during winter and spring would be appealing. The musical splashing of a small fountain or waterfall creates a restful, intimate atmosphere, as well as masking background noise.

■ *Gardening.* Do you like to weave a natural tapestry and create visual effects with flowers and foliage? Or are you more interested in growing the kind of herbs, fruits, and vegetables that are always so much tastier than store-bought ones?

■ *Entertaining.* If you like to give big parties, bench-railings along the sides of a deck will provide seating for large numbers of people. In contemplating your

Small trees or shrubs in built-in planters screen a sitting area.

Canvas shades can be adjusted to your desire for privacy.

Translucent plastic provides privacy with plenty of light.

Preassembled reed screens tacked on a frame.

design, be sure to check out traffic patterns; your guests should be able to move freely about the garden and in and out of the house without running into dead-end routes or being continually confronted by bottle-necks. Would an entertainment area by the poolhouse or at the end of the patio make your entertaining easier and more pleasant?

■ *Cooking and dining.* If you like to cook outdoors, think about constructing a barbecue center with a built-in grill, storage for equipment, supplies, and dishes, an electrical outlet, and perhaps even a sink. This can be incorporated into a corner of the patio; doing both in brick would add unity to the design. (Outdoor cooking surfaces can also double as potting areas for container plants.) A dining table and chairs or benches can be conveniently placed nearby. Unless you have a complete outdoor entertaining area, locate the dining area as close to the indoor kitchen as you can, to make it easier to serve from there.

PRIVACY WITHIN THE GARDEN

Since their invention, gardens in every culture and country have been associated with the idea of seclusion. Most of us today are in no less need of a retreat than our ancestors were. As you plan your back yard garden, you might want to create a special spot for seclusion. Areas that are tucked away and not immediately apparent also lend an air of mystery to the garden.

You'll probably want to site your retreat away from the house, away from the routines of everyday life. Does a gazebo at the end of the garden sound beguiling? It can be as grand or as simple as you like, a Victorian jewel or a rough wooden structure. If your backyard is large enough, you could add a "false bottom"; the garden would appear to end, but beyond the initial boundary another small garden would offer safe haven. Be sure not to make a "secret garden" so small that it induces claustrophobia; pace off and sketch the

The back yard of the base plan takes on a new look. The fence on the two sides that have particular privacy problems is augmented by a row of large trees on the right, and an aerial hedge rising above the fence on the left. The masonry wall at the back gives maximum protection against car lights, noise, and litter. A lattice arbor on one side of the hot tub off the master bedroom provides privacy and a sense of enclosure. The same functions are performed by shrubs in containers flanking the sunbathing area to the right of the pool. A large tree in the left corner provides welcome shade for the arbor that incorporates a poolside dressing room.

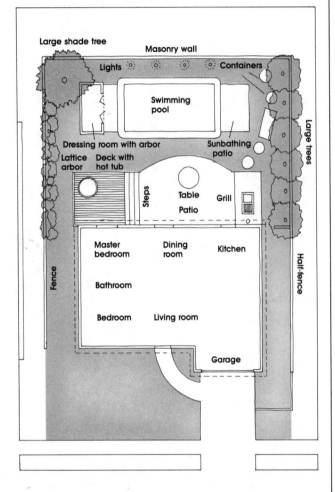

dimensions carefully. On the other hand, children love tiny secret gardens; consider a child-size hideaway in a secluded corner for private afternoon tea parties.

Less elaborate but still effective in creating private places is to use peninsula and island flower beds to break up an expanse of lawn and create nooks and crannies. Peninsula beds jut into the lawn and provide a place for plants to screen the lawn beyond. Island beds are surrounded on all sides by lawn and, judiciously planted, can block views to the farther reaches of the garden. These beds can be planted with just shielding shrubbery, or they can also include annuals and perennials.

What could be more romantic than an old-fashioned rose bower? Constructed of timber and lath or pipe and wire, the bower can accommodate a pair of benches. If you live in zone 7 or higher, consider two evergreen (or semi-evergreen, depending on the winter cold) climbing roses; both are fairly fast-growing and will cover your framework in a short time. 'Climbing Cecile Brunner' (also called Sweetheart Rose) has fine light green foliage and a profusion of small, somewhat fragrant, bright pink blossoms in the spring with lesser periods of bloom in the summer and fall. Lady Banks' rose (*Rosa banksiae*) has darker foliage, and has two generally available cultivars: 'Alba Plena' with double white flowers that smell like violets, and 'Lutea' with double scentless creamy-yellow flowers. If you prefer larger-flowered roses, refer to the Sunset book *How to Grow Roses* for further information on available varieties.

HOT TUBS AND SWIMMING POOLS

Screens and fences are a good bet for providing privacy around pools and spas, with container plants and vines to brighten corners and soften the lines. Screens and fences also provide welcome air circulation on hot days. Lattice screens are a natural solution for providing visual privacy with good air circulation, while fences can be baffled or louvered to allow air currents to pass through.

Hot tubs, spas, and swimming pools demand a high degree of privacy, and pose some special problems and constraints when it comes to landscaping around them.

■ *Litter.* Anyone who has tediously fished leaves, seed pods, and other debris out of a swimming pool can testify to the wisdom of planting "neat" trees and shrubs in the vicinity. You have a little more leeway around hot tubs as they usually include covers for heat retention. Also, a roof is more feasible over a hot tub than over a swimming pool. Stay away from plants that bear fruits or berries around tubs or pools; they can make decking or paving slick, and will leave unsightly stains. (Also keep in mind that fruits start with flowers, and flowers attract bees—not the kind of guests you want to invite to your swimming pool.)

■ *Drainage.* Paving is graded away from the tub or pool, so runoff from rain or hosings will tend to drain into the surrounding flower beds. Depending on how large the paved areas are, you'll need to channel the runoff away from the beds or provide extra drainage in the beds themselves. Raised beds will also protect plantings against drowning. Using decking instead of paving can reduce the concentration of drainage to certain areas.

■ *Humidity.* The constant evaporation of water from a tub or pool raises the moisture content of the surrounding air considerably. If your climate allows, this makes subtropical and tropical plants a natural, but unless you have good air circulation, plants that are at all susceptible to mildew should be avoided. An extensive list of plants that are happy near pools can be found in the Sunset book *Ideas for Swimming Pools.*

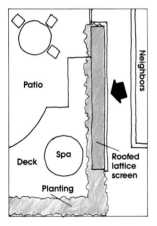

PLANTS AND STRUCTURES FOR PRIVATE BATHING

These backyard sitting and bathing areas (sketch above) are protected by a lattice screen placed in front of a low fence and a leafy surround of shrubs and small trees. The photo at top shows the low deck around the hot tub, with the view toward the lattice screen. The photo at right shows the view from the sitting area toward the tub. Design: John Bernhard, Seattle, WA.

Sketch labels: Neighbors, Patio, Deck, Spa, Planting, Roofed lattice screen

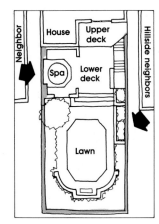

A MULTILEVEL INTEGRATION OF HOUSE AND GARDEN

A major problem faced by the owners of the San Francisco garden pictured on this page was how to join the living areas of the house with those of the garden. The design solution is shown in the sketch at left.

A small deck was built off the main floor. The view from this deck is shown in the photo at left center. Colorful summertime plantings of sweet alyssum, impatiens, hydrangeas, and hybrid lilies frame the view across the garden. The large *Eucalyptus ficifolia* screens the view of adjacent neighbors.

Stairs lead to a lower deck a few steps above ground level (photo below). A tall Japanese maple in a large container ties the deck to the garden.

The perimeter of the garden is planted with winter-blooming camellias that maintain their handsome foliage year-round against the fence, which was shingled to match the house (photo bottom left). Containers and interplantings of annuals keep the garden colorful all year. Design: Johnson Guthrie Associates, San Francisco, CA; Horticultural Consultant: Stephen Marcus, San Francisco, CA.

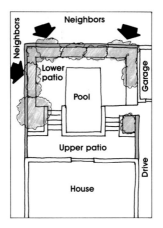

TALL HEDGES BLOCK WIND AND VIEWS

Tall, informally trimmed hedges provide a wind-break and privacy to the back yard pool shown in the photo below and in the sketch at left. The top of the hedge is kept trimmed so that the view from the upper terrace will not be blocked. Design: Robert Fletcher, West Los Angeles, CA.

A TREE SCREENS POOL FROM CHURCH ACROSS THE STREET

The back yard pool shown in the photo at right is shielded from the view of the church across the street by a tall weeping willow. Aligning the pool with the existing tree created a strong and effective design composition. Design: Oehme van Sweden Associates, Washington, DC.

Around almost any home you can find a number of places that are little used because they lack privacy and a pleasant ambience. Side yards, rooftops, and balconies are often underused because they aren't comfortable, and that discomfort is frequently the result of being exposed to the view of the world.

In addition to lacking privacy, most such areas are so small and oddly shaped that it's difficult to see how it's possible to get any use out of them at all. Often, however, such a design challenge will elicit an imaginative solution that seems so natural that only you will know how useless the area was before. This section explores solutions to some common problem areas, presents ideas for tapping their hidden potentialities in order to create outdoor living spaces, and briefly discusses the special needs of plants in containers.

SIDE YARDS

Side yards are usually long and narrow—perhaps as narrow as 6 feet in width, running the full length of the house—hemmed in on one side by the house and on the other by a 6-foot fence. And if the neighbor's bedroom window looks down into the area from a few feet away, the side yard seems to be completely unusable. How do you even start to think about transforming it into an attractive, inviting space?

BACK TO THE BASICS

Refer back to the plan you made of your house and garden to gather some vital statistics on the problem area. This information will help you plan what sort of landscaping will be most useful in the side yard.

What exposure does the side yard have? If it's a northern exposure it will probably be shady most of the year, which will preclude certain activities and planting schemes. On the other hand, if the yard has a southern exposure it will likely be warm much of

the year and you may wish to add overhead protection to keep the area and the house cooler during the hot summer months. An eastern exposure may provide a site for early morning coffee, and a western orientation the perfect spot for a predinner chat.

SIDE YARD BASE PLAN

On the left of the sample plan, the aerial hedge that began in the back yard has been extended along the fence. Across the walkway, narrow beds are planted with an assortment of vegetables. Because the exposure is to the south, a greenhouse window insert will not shade the bed below. In the right side yard, which gets less sun, keep the planting simple with a hedge of shade-tolerant shrubs.

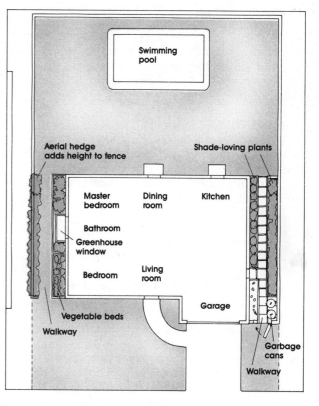

Swimming pool

Aerial hedge adds height to fence

Shade-loving plants

Master bedroom

Dining room

Kitchen

Bathroom

Greenhouse window

Bedroom

Living room

Garage

Vegetable beds

Walkway

Garbage cans

Walkway

Opposite: A comfortable corner of an urban roof garden. All the plants are grown in containers, including the wisteria overhead, the chrysanthemums, left, and the impatiens, right. Design: Cole-Wheatman Interior Designers, San Francisco, CA.

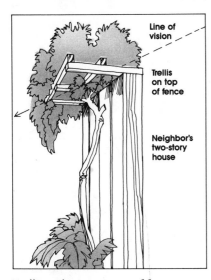

Trellis with vine on top of fence blocks neighbors' view into side yard.

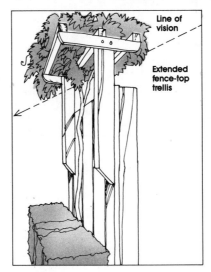

Trellis with vine extended above fence blocks view of yard and window.

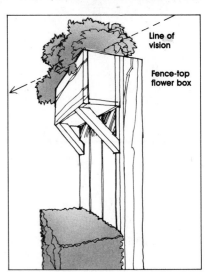

Box attached to top of fence and planted with bushy annuals adds color to yard.

What rooms of the house give on to the side yard? Looking at the indoor living spaces adjacent to the side yard may inspire you about the kind of garden you can create to complement or expand the indoor area. Perhaps there's room for a small patio for after-dinner coffee off the dining room. Or think of a small greenhouse right off the bathroom, or a restful oriental-style minigarden outside the bedroom window.

Consider also the amount of additional privacy that landscaping in the side yard can provide the interior rooms of the house. If your bedroom seems stuffy because you always keep the blinds drawn for privacy, landscaping can often allow you to have both an open window and privacy.

DEALING WITH ODD SHAPES

In dealing with a long side yard, there are two basic options you can consider, depending on the width of the space. If the side yard is very narrow, say 6 feet or so, you're probably stuck with working with the space and creating a long, linear design. If the width of the side yard is greater—say 12 feet—then you may be able to visually or physically break up the space into shorter compartments.

Working with the space. If you want to maintain the long, narrow perspective, you might attach a trellis to the fence and grow trailing vines along the top to shield the area from the neighbor's view. Or, if the building codes in your area allow it, consider extending the height of the fence with a latticework screen. For more complete overhead privacy, a pergola the length and breadth of the yard is an attractive structure on which to train vines or to hang colorful container plants.

In a small area like a side yard, unity in the design is especially important. If you're planting shrubs, use the same kind of shrub throughout. Or establish a

theme by using only gray foliage plants. Vines planted on a trellis along the fence might be echoed by vines on latticework against the house. One effective way of treating such an area is to give it a focus: a single specimen tree or shrub at one or both ends of the yard will draw the eye and provide a visual framework for the narrow progression of the other plantings. Such a focus might also be a structure, such as an arched wall that gives just a glimpse of the back yard garden beyond and invites exploration.

Breaking up the space. If your side yard is relatively wide, breaking the long area up into smaller "rooms" gives greater versatility in the use of the space, although care must be taken not to chop up the space into areas that are so small that they become uncomfortable and unusable.

You can divide such a space with structures, like screens, walls, or fences; or with plantings of tall perennials, shrubs, or hedges. Using identical or at least similar means of dividing the spaces will unify your design and lessen the possibility that the sequence of areas will seem choppy.

Relate each of the sequence of gardens to the adjacent room of the house. For example, if you want to have a workbench for potting chores, that might go next to the garage. An herb garden might be outside the kitchen, with trailing rosemary cascading from a planter box attached to the top of the fence. You might design the area off the dining room with simple brick paving surmounted by a rustic pergola with a canopy of morning glory or jasmine for overhead privacy.

If your side yard is wide enough, a greenhouse is an excellent way to create a particularly lovely kind of private spot. Several manufacturers now offer modular units that are easy to install right into the side of the house. The lush growth of the plants will provide ample

A relatively wide side yard can be broken into two or three separate small gardens or activity areas.

A long, narrow, sunny side yard can be used as a vegetable garden with the main path in the center and access paths.

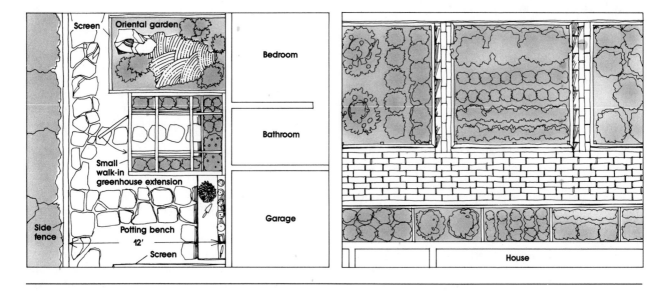

privacy. Bathrooms are particularly good candidates for greenhouse extensions. Screening or a coat of whitewash will provide privacy, and the high humidity of the bathroom will be appreciated by the plants. If you can't afford a whole greenhouse room, or if the side yard is too narrow to accommodate it, consider a greenhouse window insert that projects only 18 or 24 inches from the house. You will still have the benefit of light in the room, and the plants will effectively screen the view from the outside.

PLANTING SIDE YARDS

Because side yards are often isolated from the rest of the garden and its outdoor living spaces, you can create a different theme or emphasis in this part of your garden. This is an excellent area in which to cultivate specialty plants or, if you're a collector, to group the plants of your particular enthusiasm. It's often desirable to have vegetable gardens out of sight of the main garden since they have periods when they look unkempt. Flowers grown for cutting can be efficiently cultivated in a long, narrow bed. Or a collection of succulents and cacti can be nurtured along the side of the house where they will not look out of context with the rest of the garden design.

You'll want to choose plants that match the small scale of the side yard. This rules out most trees, although smaller trees, such as Japanese maple and crabapple, can often be accommodated in a narrow space. Make sure that the plants you choose can take the conditions in the side yard. A shady, cool, north-facing side yard may be a perfect place for ferns and aucuba. On the other hand, a south-facing side yard will trap a good deal of heat during the summer months, making it ideal for sun and heat-loving plants, such as citrus or rockroses.

HIDING UTILITY AREAS

It's an unfortunate fact that most homes and gardens have areas that are best hidden from view. Garbage cans, dog runs, swimming pool and spa pumps, compost heaps, and tool sheds can strike a discordant note in a handsome, well-groomed garden. When you are designing your landscape, be sure to integrate screens within the garden to hide the view of unsightly areas.

What kind of visual barrier you use—shrubs, hedges, fences, or walls—will be largely determined by the sorts of barriers that already exist in your garden. If the unity of the landscape design is cleverly maintained, the finished design will give no clue that a particular hedge or fence hides an unattractive object or area.

Sometimes requirements will dictate a different type of barrier than you have used in other parts of the garden; a chain link fence to pen a dog, for instance, when all other areas of the garden use cedar fencing. You might go so far as to build a cedar fence in front of the chain link fence; or you could highlight the difference by covering the chain link with fast-growing ivy. A couple of small trellises covered with ivy against the cedar fence would tie your over-all design together.

ROOF GARDENS

In many urban and suburban areas where space is at a premium, the roof is the only place where it's possible to have a garden. Slope dwellers also often resort to rooftops as the only level outdoor area available to them. However, unless you're at the top of the tallest building around, your roof garden will be exposed to the gaze of the neighbors, so your planning must include provisions for shelter and privacy.

In most cases you can immediately eliminate walls as candidates for privacy barriers; masonry is usually too heavy to be supported by the structure beneath.

If you have mature trees that screen the roof, you're in luck; otherwise, trees planted in containers are probably your best bet. For rooftop trees to grow in containers, your choice will probably be limited to such small trees as Japanese maple, eastern dogwood, or dwarf fruit trees. It's not so much the size of the tree that limits its use on a rooftop, but rather the amount of soil it needs to flourish—soil is heavy, especially when it's wet. Before you design a lavish roof garden, consult a structural engineer to ascertain the maximum load the roof can take.

Shrubs in containers can block parts of the view and provide green accents on your rooftop. A tub of bamboo is an undemanding plant that will provide you with a fine-textured screen of foliage all year round. Another favorite evergreen shrub is the rhododendron, which presents handsome dark green foliage and colorful flower displays in late spring. You can even screen the view with the smaller varieties of box or holly in containers securely anchored along the railing of the rooftop.

Fences and screens provide the greatest degree of privacy. If the privacy barrier must also serve as a windbreak, a wooden wall is probably the best solution. But don't construct a solid wall to shield yourself from wind. A screen that allows the passage of some wind through it breaks up the breeze into smaller eddies, while a strong wind will simply wash over a solid barrier with no reduction in its force.

Many different kinds of materials and designs are appropriate for a roof garden fence: boards for a solid screen, lattice made from 1 by 1's or lath, canvas laced to a frame, delicate reed or bamboo screening, or fiberglass panels that will let in the sunlight. Your choice of materials is limited only by your imagination, the weight of the materials, the strength of the wind, and the need for visual integration with the surroundings.

Overhead, a trellis or pergola covered with vines is a charming way to provide both privacy and shade. Leave some of the overhead area uncovered to let in a spot of sun for sun-loving plants and people.

Be selective in your determination of where you need privacy protection and where you don't, so that you don't end up with an enclosed, hemmed-in feeling. It's a simple matter to design and construct windows in your enclosures so that you can take advantage of a special view, or to pick a design—such as open latticework covered by vines—that will let air and light into the roof garden.

DECKS AND BALCONIES

Decks and balconies above ground level are subject to the same restrictions, and can use many of the same methods of providing privacy, as roof gardens. A well-placed shrub or small tree can block a view onto the deck, or a box along the balcony railing can be planted with a small hedge or a colorful mass of annuals. Woven screens of reed or bamboo, or slats of lath, can be attached to railing posts to provide privacy from below.

If your deck faces another house whose side windows look directly onto it, a solid screen or fence at that end will block the view. Or consider a vertical-louvered screen that will allow you to look through, but won't allow the neighbors to see in.

GARDENING IN CONTAINERS

Although container plants are particularly useful to provide privacy in rooftop gardens and on decks and balconies, they are of course adaptable to any part of the garden. Annuals in containers provide splashes of color around patios, alongside stairways, or inside the house. Frost-tender plants such as citrus can be enjoyed in cold-winter climates when grown in containers that allow them to be moved to a protected spot. For complete information, see the Sunset book *Gardening in Containers*.

PLANTS FOR CONTAINER GARDENING

In theory, just about any plant can be grown in a container if the root system has enough soil in which to grow. In practice, the maximum practical size and weight of the container limits your choice to most annuals and perennials and small trees and shrubs. Because the root systems of larger shrubs and trees planted in containers are constricted, their top growth will be smaller than if they were planted in the ground. A root pruning or repotting into a slightly larger container every three to five years will keep the plants healthy.

TYPES OF CONTAINERS

Just about anything that will hold soil and drain water can be used as a planting container. Wooden tubs or boxes are excellent, as are the common terra cotta pots, although water evaporates quickly from the latter. Plastic pots retain water better, although they are somewhat less handsome. Metal cans work well unless the container is in full, hot sun, in which case the roots can get cooked. No matter what kind of container you use, if it sits in full sun on a surface that absorbs heat, such as concrete, put the container on a stand to allow air to circulate beneath it.

WATERING AND FEEDING

Watering is the most frequent necessary chore you'll have to perform. In the ground, plants have a large amount of soil from which to draw moisture and nutrients. The limited amount of soil in containers means that the moisture in the soil must be replenished often. When the weather is hot, dry, or windy, you may have to water small containers every day.

Monthly feedings of a diluted mixture of general-purpose liquid fertilizer are generally sufficient to keep your container plants growing vigorously.

Almost all plants appreciate good drainage so that their soil is not constantly soggy. All containers must have drainage holes, and most plants will benefit from a layer of gravel or broken crockery in the bottom of the pot. If you use a saucer or tray beneath your container plants, be sure the pots are not standing in the runoff water.

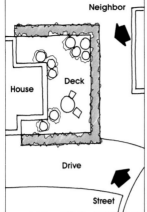

PRESERVING A VIEW

A rooftop deck (left, sketch above) affords a sweeping view; the neighbors also have a good view of the deck. But a hedge of Japanese holly in boxes along the railing provides privacy to the deck while preserving the view. Design: David Poot, Seattle, WA.

SHELTERED OUTDOOR ROOMS

Parts of this roof deck, below, are covered by fiberglass panels that admit sunlight but keep out the rain and views from the neighbors. Design: David Poot, Seattle, WA.

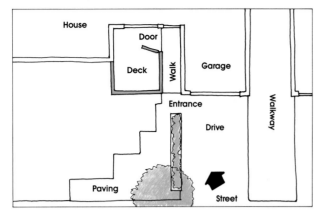

House				
	Door			
	Deck	**Walk**	**Garage**	
		Entrance		**Walkway**
			Drive	
Paving				
			Street	

TREES AND A SCREEN PROVIDE A BUFFER

A lattice screen and open, airy overhead protect the front and side of the house shown in the photo below. As the sketch above shows, a generous pathway leads from the front garden to the back. Design: Don Boos, Los Altos, CA.

BAMBOO HEDGE FOR TOTAL PRIVACY

The small side yard shown at right is a pleasant sitting and dining area with brick paving and an almost impenetrable hedge of bamboo. Views of the front yard of this home can be found on page 19. Design: Lani Berrington and Mario Mathias, Manhattan Beach, CA.

UGLY GARBAGE CANS WON'T INTRUDE ON THIS GARDEN

You'll have to hunt to find the garbage can in this garden, even though the photo at left focuses on its hiding place. It has its own discreet enclosure made from cedar, the same fencing material used in the rest of the garden. The gate to the left gives garbage collectors access from the alleyway beyond.

A repetitive tall column of ivy provides a backdrop for a bit of statuary on a pedestal that provides a focal point and distracts the eye from the utility area behind it. Garden of Margaret Alexander, VA.

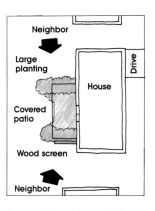

SHRUBS AND TREES FOR SECLUSION

The suburban home shown in the photo below and the sketch above is surrounded by lawn. To create a private outdoor sitting area, the owners planted a thick grouping of shrubs and trees on one side of the paved area and built a wooden screen softened by shrubs on the other side. Design: Sabina Mueller, Sulgrove, OH.

S H R U B S   A N D   H E D G E S

Shrubs are just about the most versatile group of plants the gardener has to design with. They range in size from low-growing ground covers all the way up to 15-foot-high sprawling bushes. (The top height of 15 feet is somewhat arbitrary, but plants taller than that are usually considered trees.) Some shrubs, such as roses and rhododendrons, are noted for their profusion of spectacular flowers; some, like the yew and box, for their handsome foliage; and others, such as pyracantha and cotoneaster, for their colorful berries.

Hedges are simply shrubs that have been trained or clipped to form a solid barrier or define a boundary. Unclipped shrubs may be thought of as having three dimensions: height, breadth, and mass. Although hedges also have three dimensions, their primary emphasis in garden design is their height and forming an unbroken line along their breadth.

Besides transforming shrubs into a linear barrier, clipping is also a means of increasing the density of the planting. Trimming the growing shoots on either side of the hedge encourages the growth of the shrubs toward each other, knitting the plants into a continuous row that can effectively block the view into or out of your garden.

SHRUBS AND HEDGES FOR PRIVACY

Once again, it's important to think about your needs for privacy in particular areas of your garden. Must the plant barrier be solid, or is a light screen all that is needed? If you wish merely to diffuse a direct view from the street to your front door, then a large open shrub like rhododendron may be just what you need. But if you want to completely block the view of your outdoor sitting area that abuts your neighbor's swimming pool, a closely sheared privet hedge may be your best bet.

Shrubs can be either deciduous or evergreen. What kind of shrubs you choose will depend on whether

privacy is desirable all year round or just during the growing season. A back yard patio that isn't used during the cold, wet winter months could be sheltered during spring through fall by a planting of lilacs, which lose their leaves during the winter. For screening a view into a bedroom window, though, a fast-growing evergreen would be preferable.

SHRUBS ON THE BASE PLAN

This sample plan illustrates the various ways shrubs and hedges can be used in different parts of the garden. In the front, a curved hedge encloses a sitting area, a lower hedge defines the left property boundary, and low-growing ground cover shrubs define the driveway. An aerial hedge along the left boundary line adds height to an existing fence. A line of informally trimmed shrubs softens the masonry wall at the back, and waist-high shrubs separate the pool area from the rest of the garden.

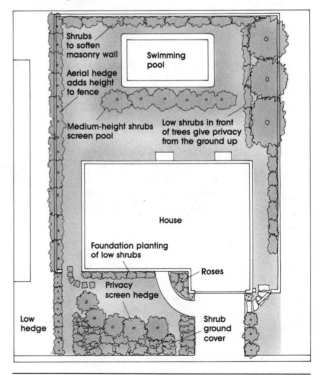

Shrubs to soften masonry wall

Swimming pool

Aerial hedge adds height to fence

Medium-height shrubs screen pool

Low shrubs in front of trees give privacy from the ground up

House

Foundation planting of low shrubs

Roses

Privacy screen hedge

Low hedge

Shrub ground cover

Opposite: Hedges sculpted into shapes, called *topiary*, can provide a focus for attention as well as a barrier. Another view of this elegant entry court can be found on page 44. Design: Thomas Church, San Francisco, CA.

When you consider the existing structures and plantings in your garden, think in terms of the vertical design of your garden as well as the horizontal. Trees often act as focal points in the garden, and can provide a screen to block your view of distant visual blights. Shrubs, on the other hand, grow to a more human scale, and can help to relate the height and bulk of trees to the garden as a whole. The starkness of solid walls and fences can be softened by plantings of small-scale shrubs. Or if zoning restrictions limit the height of a wall or fence, their height can be augmented by taller-growing shrubs.

If mature trees shade your garden, be sure to choose shrubs such as *Aucuba japonica* or camellias that do well in shade.

The style and ambience of your house and garden should also be a factor in your plans. Massing large and small untrimmed shrubs can give your garden a sense of wild, untamed nature, while neatly shaped and clipped hedges have a much more formal appearance.

MASSING SHRUBS

Trees may function as focal points in a landscape, but it is usually shrubs that provide organization and a sense of enclosure, and that give a garden design its form and structure. In fact, you might think of shrubs as the "skeleton" of the garden.

Shrubs offer a tremendously wide and varied palette. You have a choice of leaf textures, growth habits and shapes, leaf colors in the growing season as well as autumn, and flower color and display. In fact, you may have to restrain yourself from choosing too many different varieties for your garden. Because shrubs are such strong structural elements, you'll want to maintain unity in your design by limiting your selections to a few species and varieties. Try to keep the same varieties together in clumps or stretches. If the same shrubs are

dotted all over the garden, the eye will be busily drawn from one to another, leading to a choppy effect and cheating the shrubs of their chance to shine.

Think also of unity over time. You may wish to choose evergreen shrubs for your major plantings so that you will have a green backdrop throughout the year. This constant backdrop will give you visual privacy all year round, and can be enlivened with plantings of annuals and perennials during the growing season. Deciduous shrubs can be used along with the evergreens as accents for their flowers, their autumn foliage, or their interesting winter forms.

Like all plants, shrubs need plenty of room to grow. To ensure the future health of your shrubs, avoid the temptation to overplant, and be sure to take seriously the mature dimensions of your plants. Public parks and botanical gardens will have mature specimens of shrubs to help you judge their ultimate size. Overcrowded shrubs will have a difficult time attaining their natural form and shape. Besides, intertwined shrubs look messy and are hard to control.

If you're planting other shrubs or large plants in front of a hedge, allow 12 to 18 inches or even more between the hedge and the foreground plantings. This access is important when the hedge needs clipping; it allows some visual depth between the foreground and the hedge; and the play of light and shadow against the hedge can be very attractive.

CHOOSING SHRUBS FOR YOUR LANDSCAPE

As you read through the list of shrubs on page 42, keep in mind the following characteristics, and your particular requirements for privacy.

GROWTH RATE

Some shrubs grow much more rapidly than others. Your first impulse may be to go with the shrubs that grow quickly so that you'll have your privacy screen

AN AERIAL HEDGE

Where zoning regulations restrict height, an aerial hedge can give added height while still allowing room for lower shrubs and bedding plants.

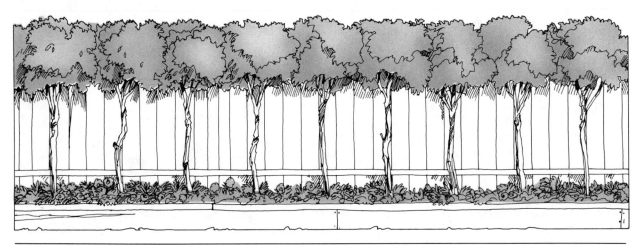

as soon as possible. Tempting as that may be, don't forget the maintenance that fast-growing shrubs will require after they have grown to their mature height. To keep them from getting leggy (losing their lower branches so that the main stems show) or completely out of control, you will have to prune or clip them back frequently. Unless you have the time and the inclination to perform this maintenance, you're better off with the slower-growing varieties.

Don't despair if the shrub touted as "moderately fast growing" seems to have a snaillike growth rate the first year after you plant it. Most shrubs take time to get established; they're concentrating on setting up a strong root system to nourish the plant before sending out extensive growth above ground. After the first two or three years, most shrubs will reward you with steady growth.

You can interplant fast-growing varieties of shrubs among the slow growers, but in that case the fast growers will probably have to be severely trimmed or taken out completely just as they are becoming full-fledged specimens. Instead, think about temporarily filling in any gaps in your landscape with tall quick-growing annuals and perennials, such as cosmos, foxgloves, sunflowers, or hollyhocks.

FOLIAGE

Leaf color, foliage texture and density, and whether the plant is deciduous or evergreen—all of these factors contribute to the visual effect of the shrubs in your garden. Where privacy is your primary concern, you'll probably want to check to see if the shrub is evergreen or deciduous, how densely the foliage grows, and the "subordinate" qualities of foliage texture and color.

Evergreen versus deciduous. Evergreen shrubs are the best choice for the basic structure of your hedges, although where privacy is not a particular concern during the winter, other attributes may be more important. Deciduous shrubs that provide especially fine displays of flowers or autumn foliage are good for accents or emphasis.

Foliage density. The density of the foliage is of particular concern when you are planting for privacy. If you are simply trying to break up a view, a solid barrier may not be necessary. However, if you want to block a view completely, choose a shrub whose foliage grows thickly, such as box, elaeagnus, or yew. When choosing hedge plants, keep in mind that repeated trimming on the top and outsides will stimulate growth to the sides, resulting in denser growth than in an untrimmed plant.

Foliage texture. Many garden designers consider foliage texture to be one of the most important considerations in selecting garden plants. The visual effect of small crinkled leaves is very different from that of large, smooth-edged, glossy leaves. In general, small-leafed shrubs are suited to small gardens, while large-leafed shrubs are best used sparingly or for large expanses of shrubbery or hedges. Small-leafed hedges are easier to keep trimmed because they can be sheared. Large-leafed hedges develop a ragged look when sheared and are better trimmed one branch at a time, a more time-consuming process.

Leaf color. Shrubs vary in color from light to dark green, with shades of gold to bronze, and variations of gray provided by the undersides of leaves in some varieties. Some varieties have variegated, multi-colored foliage that provides intriguing splashes of yellow or white. Once again, resist the temptation to plant one specimen of each color you like, but strive for a unified look enlivened by accents. Use different colored foliage in bursts, at transitional points as the landscaping changes from one part of the garden to another, or as the focus of a particularly spectacular display. Use shrubs of different colors to define different areas of your garden, but aim for a subtle, natural change so the effect is not jarring and the areas don't compete with one another.

TRIMMING HEDGES

Side view: Trim hedges wider at the bottom so that lower leaves will not be shaded by those above.

Front view: Pruning the sides along the length of the hedge will encourage growth to fill in between the shrubs.

A SELECTION OF SHRUBS

The following list is just a sampling of the many shrubs from which you can choose as you are designing your landscape for privacy. The plants listed here cover a broad range of climate zones. Some are evergreen, some deciduous, many can be clipped into hedges, and some will reward you with glorious flowers as well as a leafy screen.

Aucuba japonica. This evergreen shrub, good for zones 7 through 10, thrives in shade and tolerates poor soil well. It's an excellent choice massed on the north side of a house as a privacy screen. Densely growing at a moderate rate to a height of 10 feet with almost as great a spread, Japanese aucuba has large leaves that should be clipped back rather than sheared. Many varieties have white or yellow variegated leaves.

Bamboo. These fast-growing evergreen grasses can give you a finely textured but dense screen very quickly. Zones vary by species; most require mild winters. Beware of the types that spread by underground stems—they are invasive, and can overrun the garden. The clump-forming types can be planted as a hedge that will grow to 16 feet tall. The height can be kept under control with an annual pruning.

Buxus (Box, boxwood). This is the plant that is most often clipped into formal hedges. English boxwood (*B. sempervirens*) has small, dark green, glossy leaves that can be sheared to almost any shape you desire. Growing at a moderate rate, the species can reach 15 to 20 feet. Suitable for zones 5 through 10 in the West and zones 5 through 9 in the East, this species does not do well in alkaline soils or where summers are hot.

Camellia japonica. These elegant shrubs will provide a dark green screen throughout the year in zones 8 through 10, in addition to a spectacular display of white, pink, or red flowers from mid-autumn into spring. Different varieties are moderate to fast growing.

Chaenomeles (Flowering quince). These fast-growing deciduous shrubs for zones 4 through 9 will not provide you with much visual privacy during the winter, but their late-winter bloom in bright or pastel shades on bare branches gives a dazzling display when little else is in bloom. For the screening effect of an informal hedge, choose the upright rather than rounded varieties. Thorny stems make it a good barrier planting.

Elaeagnus. These large, fast-growing, dense, tough plants are useful for mass planting and informal hedges. The spring flowers are inconspicuous although fragrant, and are followed by small berrylike fruit. *E. commutata,* zones 1 through 7, is a deciduous species that grows to 12 feet and has silver berries. *E. pungens,* which grows to 15 feet in zones 7 through 10, is evergreen with red fruits. Thorny branches and dense growth encouraged by shearing can make this easily cared for plant an impenetrable barrier.

Ligustrum (Privet). These shrubs are widely used as sheared hedges, although they also make handsome shrubs if left to their own devices. There are both deciduous and evergreen species suitable for a wide range of climate zones. Showy white clusters of flowers appear in late spring and are followed by black berries.

Lonicera (Honeysuckle). These shrubs are not as rampant as their vining cousins, but will produce a dense, easily sheared hedge with similar sweet-smelling flowers, followed by showy fruit. The evergreen box honeysuckle (*L. nitida*) grows quickly to 6 feet in zones 7 through 10 and has glossy half-inch leaves that turn purplish in winter. Small white blossoms produce blue-purple fruit. The Tatarian honeysuckle (*L. tatarica*, zones 3 through 9), is a deciduous species that has dark green 2-inch leaves on arching stems to 9 feet high. Bright red fruit follows the small pink blossoms.

Prunus. Two species of this wide-ranging genus make excellent evergreen hedge plants. The Carolina cherry laurel (*P. caroliniana*) grows well in zones 7 through 10. It has glossy green 2-inch oval leaves, and forms dense plants to 12 feet high if left untrimmed. English laurel (*P. laurocerasus*, zones 6 through 10) has similar glossy foliage, with narrower leaves to 4 inches long.

Pyracantha (Firethorn). In zones 6 through 10, these shrubs are laden with orange to red berries from autumn through winter. Clusters of showy white flowers in late spring or early summer precede the colorful berries. Nurseries offer many different evergreen species and varieties of varying sizes, growth habits, and cold tolerances. The selection of various kinds varies regionally. Choose upright-growing varieties for both visual and protective screening.

Rhododendron (Rhododendron and azalea). This group of plants is huge, with varying sizes, cold tolerances, and flower form. Most are at least as important for their foliage as for their flowers. Massed rhododendrons will provide an imposing screen—but be sure the scale of your garden is large enough to handle them. Check with your local nursery to find out what varieties do well in your area.

Syringa (Lilac). There are many species of lilacs that work well as privacy screens with differing flower size, bloom time, and growth habit. Common lilac (*S. vulgaris*) will provide a thin screen from 15 to 20 feet high that produces thick clusters of very fragrant white, lavender, blue, purple, red, or pink flowers every spring in zones 3 through 9. In bloom they are spectacular; out of bloom and when the leaves fall, they are not so special.

Taxus (Yew). Slow-growing yews require patience of the gardener, but the reward is a dense, dark green evergreen hedge of long-lived plants that welcome a close, formal shearing. Irish yew (*T. baccata* 'Stricta', zones 6 through 9) is commonly available and will grow to a towering 20 feet. Many other species and varieties of various growth habits may be available.

Viburnum. Most viburnums are medium-size or large plants, either deciduous or evergreen, which are noted for their showy clusters of white flowers. The deciduous kinds also boast brightly colored autumn foliage. A deciduous species is the common snowball (*V. opulus* 'Roseum', zones 3 through 9), with pure white clusters of small flowers, which reaches 15 feet in height. Laurustinus (*V. tinus*), for zones 8 through 10, is an evergreen that produces white flowers from late autumn to spring on a 6 to 12-foot plant.

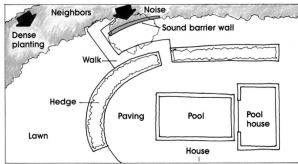

A HEDGE FOR A SENSE OF ENCLOSURE

Although the boxwood hedge in the top photograph (and indicated in the sketch above) does not directly screen the brick-paved swimming pool area from view, it provides a sense of enclosure and definition, as well as a transition to the lush green lawn. The curve of the hedge is echoed by the curve of the wooden sound barrier in the background, which is adjacent to the dense grove of trees between this property and the neighbors. Design: Morris and White, San Antonio, TX.

SHRUBS SOFTEN CONSTRUCTED BARRIERS

The back yard shown in the photo above is entirely surrounded by a grape-stake fence in the front of a screen of trees at the rear of the property. The monotony such a fence could produce if left una-dorned is alleviated by massings of spring-flower-ing azaleas and privet and the two large dwarf winged euonymus shrubs. Design: Dan Franklin, Atlanta, GA.

URBAN AND SUBURBAN PRIVACY WITH SHRUBS AND HEDGES

The photo at left shows a back yard sitting area protected by a tall, thick hedge of Canadian hemlock. Below, an urban walled entry court is brightened by evergreen box hedges (see sketch). For another view of this garden, see page 38. Design: Thomas Church, San Francisco, CA.

864

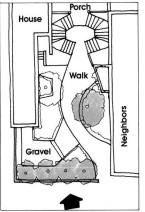

A DRAMATIC TRANSITION WITH TOPIARY

At the San Francisco Victorian home of designer Thomas Church, a pair of curving steps ascend from the front garden to the second-story entrance (see sketch above). The view from the top of the steps, left, shows how clipped balls of boxwood at different heights provide a transition from street level to the upper story.

A BAMBOO SHIELD

A hedge of bamboo almost 20 feet high, below, shields from the view of neighbors a lushly planted sitting area in the corner of a garden. Design: Lani Berrington and Mario Mathias, Manhattan Beach, CA.

If you live deep within a forest, you probably have no problem with privacy. But even if you don't have the space to surround your home with groves of trees, you can still use trees singly or in groups to ensure and enhance your seclusion.

You can use large trees to blot out a view, or smaller trees with shrubs to achieve a lush effect. Trees provide the vertical element in your garden design, while shrubs lend a lower, more horizontal feeling. Since most trees do not have branches all the way to the ground, they provide a screen from about eye level on up; for complete visual protection, use them in tandem with shrubs, fences, or walls.

Most trees will contribute more to your landscape than just privacy. They can provide shade, or brilliant fall color, or fruit. Some can withstand—and even require—freezing winters, while others enjoy baking-hot summers. Some trees retain their foliage all year round, and others let the winter sun shine through their bare branches.

With all these choices available, it's not an easy task to decide which trees will best fill your needs. This section gives you the information you need to select the trees that will best give you privacy.

USING TREES FOR PRIVACY

There are three main ways to use trees as privacy barriers around your home: plant one or two large trees to block a specific unattractive view or screen others' views into your yard; plant a small grove or group of smaller trees to screen a larger area; or plant a row of trees to achieve a hedge effect.

SINGLE SPECIMENS

Trees with a large mature size, such as Norwegian maple, coast redwood, or sycamores, need a fairly large area to grow in so they won't overwhelm their surroundings, but they will effectively block all views into

Opposite: Melaleucas shield a terrace from the neighbors' upstairs window while adding visual interest with their richly textured trunks. Design: Lin Cotton, San Francisco, CA.

and out of a large portion of your yard. If you are faced with a view of a freeway or a multistory apartment complex at the end of your lot, one or two of these trees may provide you with just the visual barrier you need. Use these sorts of trees in your landscape design with caution, however; they can cast very dense shade that makes gardening under them difficult.

TREES ON THE BASE PLAN

On the sample plan below, a cluster or grove of small trees provides shade, and perhaps flowers or fruit, as well as privacy to the front yard. Trees are also used as decorative accents and as a screen in front of the entrance, while a row of small trees along the left side breaks the view from the next-door apartment building. In the back yard, trees give privacy and shade on the two sides.

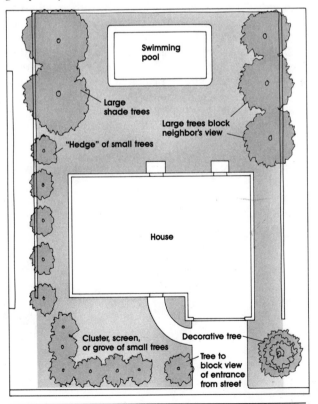

SMALL GROVES

Groupings of moderate-size or small trees, such as redbud, ginkgo, or snowball, can be placed at appropriate spots to provide shelter from the view from the neighbor's upstairs windows, or to screen undesirable views. The smaller species of these trees—particularly those with a smaller spread—give you more flexibility to design and plant around them, and they do not become major focal points that dominate the garden.

A HEDGE EFFECT

By planting a row of moderate or small-size trees you can achieve the effect of a hedge, although in most cases the screen will not grow all the way to the ground. Some trees that are good candidates for this treatment are hawthorn, crabapple, and flowering plum. You might use this kind of "hedge" along a boundary line next to your neighbor, or parallel to the property line across your front yard.

If you're willing to perform the necessary maintenance of keeping the trees topped and clipped back, you can also use larger trees as a screen. Podocarpus makes a lovely lacy screen when planted in a row. Larger faster-growing trees such as sycamore can give you a thick screen in two or three years. By heading them back at the top, and giving them a trim front and back, you will encourage the side branches to grow densely. This kind of clipping goes against the true form of the tree, so it will be a constant process, but your "hedge" will be thick and dense.

MATURE SIZE AND SHAPE

Trees grow out as well as up. The shape of a mature tree depends on the branching structure and the rate of spread relative to upward growth. There are six main categories of tree forms:

■ *Fastigate,* thin and tapering at the top and bottom, such as the Italian cypress (*Cupressus sempervirens*). A row of these could be planted to create a tall, elegant "hedge" to block or frame a view.

■ *Columnar*, the shape of a narrow cylinder, such as Lombardy poplar (*Populus nigra* 'Italica'). Trees of this shape can be planted to achieve a hedge effect; or a single specimen might block the view of a radio tower, utility pole, or other tall, slender eyesore.

■ *Cone shaped*, such as firs (*Abies* species) or coast redwood (*Sequoia sempervirens*). A small grove of these tall-growing trees will conceal any large structures beyond them.

■ *Globe*, or spherical, such as beeches (*Fagus* species). This shape lends itself best to single specimen trees.

■ *Horizontally spreading*, such as silk trees (*Albizia julibrissin*). These make admirable shade trees and provide overhead privacy.

■ *Weeping*, such as the weeping willow (*Salix babylonica*). The pendulous branches of this form can create a soft visual screen that breaks up a view rather than blocking it.

SITING TREES

Your primary criterion in the placement of a new tree in your landscape will probably be that it helps to ensure your privacy. But because trees can be such large and dominant elements in your landscape, there are other considerations about their placement that should be kept in mind.

Consider the mature size and growth habits of both the branching structure and the root system of any tree you plan to plant. Visualize trees as focal points, or at least as vertical elements or accents in your landscape. If possible, relate their structure and mass to the rest of your landscape. As newly planted trees grow, you may wish to alter smaller elements of the garden design to compensate for the increasing dominance of the new trees.

Take into account the uses of adjacent areas. A tree next to the lawn that will screen the neighbors' view might also provide useful shade, but will it be able to take the amount of water the lawn needs to survive? Remember to check your plan to see where your sewer line runs; some trees, like poplars or coast redwoods, will strangle and clog your sewer line with their roots if planted too close. The above-ground part of a tree and its root system are roughly equal in size. You can tell the approximate size and spread of the root system

TREE FORMS ■■■■■

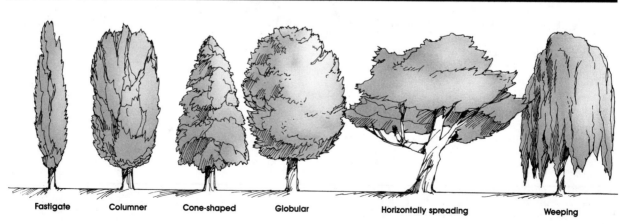

Fastigate   Columner   Cone-shaped   Globular   Horizontally spreading   Weeping

by comparing it to the branches above. The drip line of the branches defines the area of soil where the roots are concentrated.

You might want to plant a tree to hide the utility pole in the alley, but you'd better investigate the spread of any tree you choose to make sure it won't grow into the wires. Willows offer a fast-growing feathery screen, but their shallow and greedy root systems will compete with all other plants nearby. Be careful not to plant trees too close to paved walkways and patios; as the trees grow, their roots can crack the pavement.

SELECTING TREES FOR YOUR LANDSCAPE

By comparing the various attributes of a number of trees, with a little thought you'll be able to pick the ones best suited to your individual landscape.

Limit the number of different *types* of trees in favor of repeated plantings of the same species. As a design consideration, this is especially important in average-size gardens, where uniformity of foliage makes for a restful effect. You can add variety and emphasis with smaller plants.

FAST OR SLOW GROWING

Although most trees grow at a fairly moderate rate—and some of them quite slowly—there are a number of trees, such as acacias and coast redwood, that grow 3 to 4 feet a year. Such rapid growth can be very useful if you have an area that you want screened quickly. The corollary to fast growth, however, is that the trees are likely to continue at this fast clip until they completely overwhelm your garden, both above-ground and, in many cases, with their rampant root systems.

This doesn't mean that you shouldn't plant fast-growing trees in your garden to achieve a quick effect, only that you'd be wise to interplant them with slower-growing ones so that as the slower ones mature you can take out the fast growers and let the others take over.

In fact, in a completely new garden, it's not a bad idea to overplant when you first set out trees, so that you'll have a verdant grove initially. However, this technique requires you to be ruthless later on as the trees mature and they require more room to grow to achieve their proper height and shape.

FOLIAGE

One of the primary considerations in choosing a tree is whether its foliage (leaves or needles) is evergreen or deciduous. Evergreen trees will maintain a leafy screen all year. But you should think about whether that's really what you need. If you're protecting a portion of your yard that you use primarily in the summertime, perhaps the screening effect isn't necessary during the winter. Remember also that with the sun lower in the southern sky during the winter, the tree's bare branches will allow more sun to shine in the yard or on the house. If the brilliant reds, yellows, and oranges of autumn leaves, and the light, delicate greens of spring, are important to you, you'll want to choose a deciduous tree with fall coloration.

ROOT SYSTEMS

The underground root system of a tree is roughly analogous to its above-ground structure. The drip line is a handy gauge of the extent of a tree's root system.

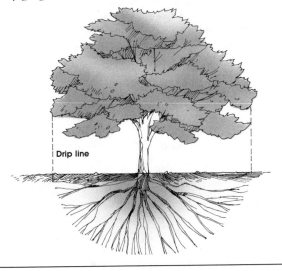

Drip line

In the autumn, the falling leaves of deciduous trees will have to be swept and gathered or allowed to mulch the flower beds. True, this can be a major job; but remember that evergreen trees don't maintain the same leaves year after year either—the constant renewal of leaves or needles accounts for a slow but steady drop of spent leaves all year round. Depending on the proximity of pools and patios, and on how much maintenance time you want to spend, this may be preferable or not.

Once you've made the basic decision about size, shape, rate of growth, and evergreen versus deciduous, you can get down to the finer points of tree selection: foliage color and leaf size. Among the practically infinite gradations of green, would you prefer light green, forest green, dark green, or blue green? Leaf size can also affect the general appearance of the tree you choose. A small-leafed tree such as a quaking aspen (*Populus tremuloides*) will give a much more delicate impression than a large-leafed tree such as sycamore (*Platanus*).

FLOWERS AND FRUIT

Many trees will give you the added bonus of flowers or fruit or both. Flowering trees can add a colorful dimension to your garden. The fruit of some trees is strictly ornamental, while other kinds have delicious fruit. Keep in mind, though, that if you want to have a good crop you'll have to put in the time pruning, spraying, watering, and harvesting. For the most part, fruiting trees belong away from living areas; the dropping fruit can be messy. If you don't want to invest the time and effort that a successful crop requires, there are many varieties of flowering fruit trees, including cherry, plum, peach, and apricot, that will give you a spectacular spring display of blossoms and produce little if any fruit.

A SELECTION OF TREES

The following list, although by no means exhaustive, offers suggestions for trees that have proved effective in providing privacy. Many of them will also add emphasis to your landscape, with a springtime display of flowers, summer shade, or brilliant fall color.

A good way to start your selection process is to visit local public or botanical gardens or an arboretum (literally "a place grown with trees") to see what kinds of trees do well in your area. This will also give you a chance to check on the mature size and effects of many trees you're interested in. It's easy to see a small tree in a nursery, or a photograph in a book, and think, "That handsome tree would be a good bet for blocking the view from the neighbor's kitchen window," only to find in a few years that the tree is completely out of scale to your garden *and* your neighbor's kitchen window.

Acer (Maple). These deciduous trees cover a large range of sizes and shapes. Most have shallow root systems that compete with other plantings; lawns and undemanding ground covers do best. Smaller varieties of maple are somewhat less greedy.

The Japanese maple (*A. palmatum*) is suitable for zones 6 through 9 in the West and 5 through 8 in the East. It grows to 20 feet high and equally wide at a moderate rate, with a multibranched trunk and rounded head that can be easily trained to a flat-topped, horizontal, oriental look. Plant singly or in small groves for a lacy screen. This tree has good autumn color in reds and yellows, and prefers partial shade to full sun.

Among the large species to be planted as specimens, red maple (*A. rubrum*) grows to 70 feet, in zones 4 through 10. Silver maple (*A. saccharinum*), zones 4 through 9, has silvery gray leaf undersides that shimmer in the breeze. Growth is upright and fast to 100 feet high and 75 feet wide, with upright limbs and somewhat drooping branches.

Albizia julibrissin (Silk tree, mimosa). A deciduous tree ranging from zones 5 through 10, the elegant flowering silk tree casts light shade, and is good for overhead privacy in a sitting area. One or more trunks rise to form a flat-topped canopy up to 40 feet high. The many small leaflets in each leaf give the foliage a feathery effect. Summertime fluffy pink to red flowers dot the top of the canopy. With regular watering, growth is rapid. This tree grows well in lawns, although litter from flowers, leaves, and seed pods can be a nuisance.

Betula (Birch). These trees are a handsome addition to the landscape all year round, providing a "polite" screen that never seems to block the view, just diffuse it. The light green foliage of spring and summer turns golden in the autumn. Plant them in groups as they appear in nature. European white birch (*B. pendula*), moderately fast growing to 40 feet high, is the species most widely planted in zones 3 through 10 in the West and 3 through 7 in the East. Other attractive species are available for different climate zones.

Crataegus (Hawthorn). The many species and varieties of these deciduous trees will grow in most zones. These are small trees to 25 feet high with dense thorny branching that develops into a thick screen. They are effective and attractive planted in a row. Single blossoms in flat clusters appear in the spring after the leaves; they are usually white, but pink and red varieties are also available. The fruit that follows in summer and fall looks like clusters of tiny red apples. Fall color is red or orange. These trees may attract aphids, and are not good near a patio or walkway.

Cupressocyparis leylandii (Leyland cypress). This evergreen conifer, adaptable to zones 5 through 10, will make an attractive, dense hedge 40 to 50 feet high in a short period of time. Its form is almost columnar, with upright branches of flattened, gray-green foliage sprays. Although it can be used as a specimen, its chief value for privacy is as a high hedge or screen plant that can be trimmed as needed.

Ilex (Holly). These slow-growing evergreens produce a dense, practically impenetrable screen. Most hollies are either male or female; females bear the colorful fruit in late autumn, but need a male tree of the same species nearby. English holly (*I. aquifolium*) is the most widely planted, good for zones 6 through 9 in the West and 6 through 8 in the East. Many varieties are available with variations in foliage or berries; most grow to 40 feet with sufficient water and good drainage.

Malus (Crabapple). There are many species and literally hundreds of varieties of this deciduous flowering tree. Winter hardiness depends on the variety. Growth is at a moderate rate from 10 to 30 feet. Before the leaves appear in the spring, you'll be treated to a display of single, semidouble, or double flowers in shades of pink to red. Many varieties also bear decorative fruit. This is an excellent colorful screening tree; a row along a boundary can present a striking view. Shade-loving plants grow well below. Prune only to train and then leave them alone.

Pinus (Pine). There are scores of different species of these needled evergreens with a broad range of growth rates, sizes and shapes, and cold tolerances. Most grow rather slowly, but some species will shoot up 8 to 10 inches a year. Rapidly growing pines for zones 7 through 10 include the Monterey pine (*P. radiata*, not good for hot summer areas) and Calabrian pine (*P. brutia*). Another fast grower, the Canary Island pine (*P. canariensis*), is suitable only for zones 9 and 10. You can shape a young tree and restrict its size to some extent, but in time the tree will defy such limitation. Your best bet in choosing a pine of the size, shape, and appearance you want is to identify those that grow naturally in your locality; or seek the advice of a nursery in your area.

Sequoia sempervirens (Coast redwood). This fast-growing (3 to 5 feet a year) evergreen conifer forms a narrow pyramid 70 to 90 feet high and 15 to 30 feet wide. A grove will form a dense screen if you have room for them. These trees also cast dense shade, which makes them difficult to garden under. They have feathery light green to gray-green foliage with small round cones, and are suitable for zones 8 through 10. Don't plant coast redwoods near a sewer line, or it will soon be strangled by the trees' powerful roots.

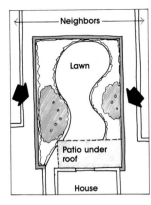

DENSE FOLIAGE PROTECTS A SMALL URBAN GARDEN

The garden shown at right (sketch above) is planted on all sides with generous stands of flowering trees. Design: Oehme, van Sweden and Associates, Washington, D.C.

AN ATTRACTIVE BONUS OF FALL COLOR

The trees that screen the front of this home in Napa, CA (below) also produce a brilliant fall display of liquidambar, birch, and Japanese maple.

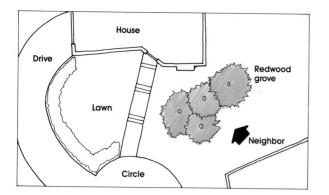

A REDWOOD GROVE PROTECTS THE FRONT OF THIS HOME

A small grove of four coast redwoods shields part of the front and the side of the home shown on this page. The sketch above shows the relationship of the closest neighbor; the trees were planted to block the view from this direction. The photo at right, top, shows the view looking across the front lawn toward the grove with its handsome dark green foliage. The photo at right, center, shows the screen of trees from the neighbors' viewpoint. Below, the view from the start of the front walk. Design: Dana Lund, Danville, CA.

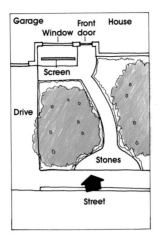

Garage Front House
  Window door
      Screen
Drive
      Stones
      Street

street (sketch at left) and enclose the space near the house. Thickly planted berms on either side of the entrance walk further define the transition from public to private space. Design: Don Boos, Los Altos, CA.

A DAZZLING SPRINGTIME SHIELD

The pink variety of a flowering dogwood shown at right shields the side yard of this Doylestown, PA, home. Younger trees in a white variety can be seen in the background; within a few years they will form a continuous "hedge." Because they are deciduous, dogwoods offer little wintertime privacy; leaves will appear just as blossoms start to fade.

A LACY SCREEN OF LEAVES GIVES PRIVACY IN FRONT

The photo below shows several clumps of birch trees that provide a leafy screen in front of a suburban home. The birches diffuse the view from the

V I N E S   A N D   C L I M B E R S

Vines are remarkably versatile plants that can be a boon to any gardener who desires privacy. The fast rate of growth of many vines makes them perfect candidates for temporary screens as well as permanent plantings. Vines and climbers are adaptable to gardens of any size. They can cover a broad area in a large garden or add their charm to a nook in a small garden. Trailing vines can even be planted in hanging containers on a small deck or balcony to shield the space from view.

Vines have a softening effect on constructed barriers such as fences, walls, and freestanding screens, and can be used to accentuate or to break up the horizontal line of these structures. Some older gardening books compared vines to the trimmings on a lady's hat: Just as no self-respecting gentlewoman would appear in an unadorned hat, they admonished, no garden structure should be bereft of the softening influence of vines that relate the structure to the rest of the garden. And in fact, the appearance of most garden structures is improved by the softening influence of vines.

Supported by a criss-cross of wires or latticework, a vine can create a leafy screen to shield you from the gaze of neighbors or passersby, or to set off or enclose different parts of the garden. Many vines, such as Virginia creeper and American bittersweet, grow so rapidly that they can cover a large expanse within a single season. Others, such as wisteria, grow more slowly; these are particularly effective grown along a high trellis and allowed to drape downward to create a light, delicate screen.

Some vines can be used to provide a dense screen for privacy, to completely cover unsightly structures, or to add height to a constructed barrier. Less rampant or less densely growing vines can be used to soften the contours of constructed barriers and to integrate them with the rest of the plantings in the garden.

Opposite: Vines can be used to accentuate architectural details of constructed barriers. An oval opaque window set in a fence for interest and symmetry is emphasized by a ring of English ivy, while a column of Burmese honeysuckle gives a vertical emphasis. The effect is formal and elegant.

TYPES OF VINES

There are literally hundreds of vines from which to choose—depending on your climate—to obliterate a view, to weave a delicate tracery on a wall or trellis, to create a spectacular display of flowers, to produce fruit, or to cast shade.

VINES ON THE BASE PLAN

Along the sides of the sample plan, vines on trellises and in planter boxes add height and soften the contours of the fences. In the front, they add visual interest to the fence that shields the front yard living space. Above the front door and over the poolside arbor in back, they provide overhead protection and enclosure. And finally, vines soften the effect of the long, plain masonry wall at the rear of the lot.

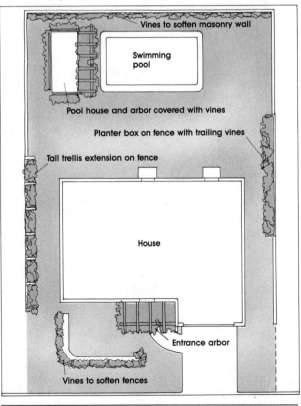

Vines to soften masonry wall

Swimming pool

Pool house and arbor covered with vines

Planter box on fence with trailing vines

Tall trellis extension on fence

House

Entrance arbor

Vines to soften fences

HOW VINES CLIMB

Before exploring some of the attributes of the versatile vines and climbers, and the uses to which they can be put, let's take a look at the ways vines climb, which determines what kind of support they need. For a plant to climb, it must have some means of supporting itself. Vines accomplish this in five different ways.

Vines that twine. Most vines have stems that grow by encircling whatever support they encounter. On fast-growing vines you can actually observe, by checking every few hours, how the stem twists and turns in its upward growth. Each plant twines in only one direction, either clockwise or counterclockwise, and should be trained so that it is able to follow that direction. The twining tendency is limited, however; the support must be fairly small (2 inches or less in diameter) for the vine to wrap around. Don't expect twining vines to encircle a large tree trunk. Some vines that twine include honeysuckle, morning glory, and wisteria.

Vines with tendrils. Tendrils are small attachments to the stem, leaf, or flower that grasp the support and hold the plant securely in place. The support given to tendrils should be thin so that it is easily grasped; narrow lath, string, or wire work well. Among the vines that use tendrils to climb are clematis, passionflower, and sweet pea.

Vines that adhere. Some vines produce small discs, rootlets, or similar attachments that cling tightly to almost any surface and support the plant as it grows. The attachment is usually very strong; they must literally be pried loose to remove them from their support. Vines that adhere in this steadfast manner include creeping fig, ivy, and Virginia creeper.

Vines with arching stems. These plants have a difficult time remaining upright when they are mature, and tend to sprawl on the ground when they are young. However, they will not perform as vines unless you train them while they are young and provide continued support by tying them to a structure while they are growing. Carolina jessamine and common jasmine are vines that require your help in growing. This group also includes climbing roses. These are not really vines, but rather shrubs that produce long canes (tough stems) that can be attached to latticework or other supports.

Vines with trailing stems. These vines are essentially ground covers, but they will grow upward if they are attached to supports. They will also follow their natural trailing habit if planted high in a container and allowed to drape downward. These trailers include lantanas and ivy geraniums.

HOW TO SUPPORT YOUR VINES

All vines need some sort of support on which to grow. The kind of support you give them depends on their method of climbing, their growth rate, and the effect you wish to achieve.

Vines that have discs or small rootlets that adhere simply need a surface on which to climb. They will clamber up a wall, fence, or tree without any assistance on your part. However, these vines must be used with

PROVIDING SUPPORT

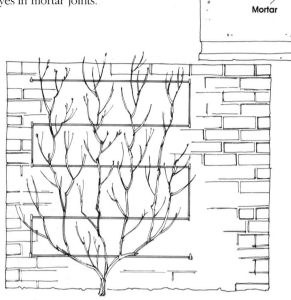

Wires strung on masonry walls can be supported by screw eyes in mortar joints.

Screw eye

Mortar

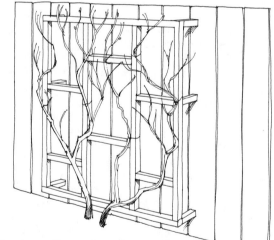

Wooden walls require a framework to support vines 2 to 3 inches from the structure for air circulation.

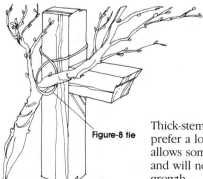

Figure-8 tie

Thick-stemmed climbers prefer a loose tie that allows some movement and will not restrict growth.

caution: Many rampant growers, such as the various kinds of ivies, can literally tear wooden or shingled structures asunder by working their way into small crevices and forcing the structure apart. Masonry walls are less susceptible to this sort of damage, but there is some evidence that the rootlets of certain vines, such as Boston ivy, may secrete an acid that can weaken the holding power of the mortar that ties a wall together.

You should also take into consideration what the structure will look like if you ever wish to remove the vine. As you pry away an adhering vine, parts of the rootlets or clinging discs will be left on the surface of the wall or structure. Removing this unattractive tracery can require many hours of scraping and scrubbing.

Care should also be taken when training evergreen vines directly on wooden structures. Wood that's covered with a constant thick mat of foliage doesn't have a chance to dry out, and will become rotten unless it's well protected. Use redwood or cedar; these woods are fairly resistant to decay. Alternatively, a screen of latticework constructed 2 or 3 inches away from the fence or other wooden structure provides "breathing room" so that air can circulate between the vine and the fence and let the wood dry out.

For vines that develop thick, woody stems, such as wisteria, be sure that the support you provide is sturdy enough. Older vines can be quite heavy, and replacing the support of a mature plant with a sturdier one is difficult and potentially dangerous to the plant. Also consider the scale of the support to the vine itself. A delicate, oriental-style fence will be better served by a lacy deciduous clematis than by a large-leafed Dutchman's pipe, which will soon engulf any subtleties of the fence design.

When tying vines to a support, use plastic gardener's tape, string, or raffia. Wire is not recommended because as the vine grows and becomes thicker, wire can cut into the stem and cut off the supply of vital nutrients. Plastic will stretch with the growth of the stem, and string and raffia will rot away before they can do any damage. Whatever material you use for ties, when you are securing fairly large and brittle stems such as rose canes, a figure-8 tie will keep the stem in place, but still allow a little movement so that the stem is less likely to snap in the wind.

EVALUATING THE ATTRIBUTES OF VINES

Like many other groups of plants, vines present a wealth of choices among their various attributes: evergreen or deciduous, annual or perennial, fruit or flowers, fast or slow growing, bushy or delicate.

EVERGREEN OR DECIDUOUS

First, evaluate your situation to decide whether it's really necessary or desirable to plant an evergreen vine for privacy. A vine-covered arbor is the perfect way to obtain some overhead privacy and a bit of shade during the summer, but it may be to your advantage to plant a deciduous vine, such as grape, so that more sunlight can penetrate during the winter. Most deciduous vines have the added attraction of colorful foliage in the fall;

An easily constructed wooden framework with wires attached by screw eyes provides support for a hedge of vines. A fast-growing vine, such as honeysuckle, will give a dense hedge in one growing season. Pinch back the primary growing shoot to encourage side shoots that will cover the area more quickly.

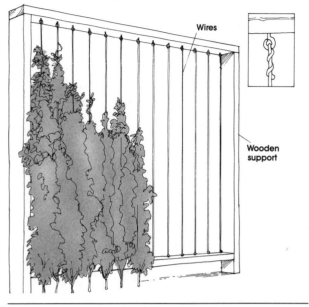

Wires

Wooden support

and the tracery of bare stems on a stone wall can be attractive during the winter as well.

ANNUAL OR PERENNIAL

Annual vines, such as sweet peas and morning glories, can quickly create a light, colorful screen from spring to autumn. They can be used to augment the screening effect of slower-growing plants, and since they die back naturally at the end of their life cycle, you need not worry about them overwhelming and stunting the growth of neighboring plants.

FLOWERS AND FRUIT

Many vines are grown primarily for their flowers or fruit, but can also serve as screen plants or adornments for privacy structures. Among those vines grown for flowers are clematis, jasmine, morning glory, rose, and wisteria. The selection of vines with edible fruit is much smaller; grapes are the most outstanding example. Pole beans, such as 'Kentucky Wonder', will create a lush annual screen with the added benefit of delicious fresh produce.

FAST OR SLOW GROWING

Most vines are relatively fast growing. As with other types of plants, your initial impulse may be to plant the fastest-growing species in order to have the most coverage in the shortest amount of time. This isn't necessarily a bad idea; however, a rampant-growing vine will continue to grow at the same rate year after year, and will require a great deal of space, as well as annual severe pruning.

A SELECTION OF VINES

The following list is only a small sampling of the kinds of vines available. It includes rampant growers that are good for filling a gap in your landscape, flowering vines for a variety of climates, and evergreen as well as deciduous vines.

***Campsis radicans* (Trumpet creeper, trumpet vine).** The hallmark of this rapidly growing deciduous vine is its spectacular display of 2-inch orange and scarlet flowers from July to September. The small leaves will form a dense cover if the growing tips are regularly pinched back during the growing season. A native of North America, it does well in zones 5 through 10.

***Celastrus scandens* (American bittersweet).** Another North American native for zones 3 through 8, this deciduous vine is good only as a temporary screen or in a large garden because its twining ropelike stems can literally strangle nearby shrubs and trees. Give it a sturdy support and prune it ruthlessly in the early spring. The light green foliage will provide a dense screen during the growing season, and the autumnal fruit capsules which split to reveal red-coated seeds make an attractive display on into the winter.

Clematis. Both evergreen and deciduous species of clematis climb by means of small tendrils attached to the leaf stems. They are not particularly rampant, but can give you an unmatched floral display.

Evergreen clematis *(C. armandii)* is a potential tree-climber, and can also be trained along the top of a wall or fence. Suitable for zones 7 through 10 in the West and 7 and 8 in the East, it will treat you to large clusters of fragrant, starlike white flowers up to 2½ inches wide against glossy dark green leaves in the early spring.

Anemone clematis *(C. montana)* is a charming deciduous species for zones 6 through 10 in the West and 6 through 8 in the East. It grows fairly rapidly into a bushy mass of bronzy green foliage covered with 2-inch pink blossoms in the spring. It will add height to a fence or wall, or trail gracefully from a trellis.

***Hydrangea anomala* (Climbing hydrangeas).** Once it is established, this deciduous vine (zones 4 through 9 in the West, and 4 through 8 in the East) can climb to great heights by means of rootlike holdfasts. Growth is slow initially, but then becomes very rapid; the vine can quickly cover a large area. It is grown primarily for its large flat white flower clusters, which contrast with the bright green leaves in midsummer.

***Ipomoea tricolor* (Morning glory).** This twining vine is an easily grown, rapidly growing (to 10 or 15 feet) annual that can provide you with a quick light screen, whether growing up a lightweight wire or plastic mesh, or trailing from an overhead trellis. The large, heart-shaped leaves contrast with the showy, funnel-shaped flowers in blue, white, lavender, pink, or red.

***Lathyrus odoratus* (Sweet pea).** This is another annual vine that provides a quick light cover with the added benefit of brilliant, fragrant flowers in almost as many shades as the rainbow. The vines climb by means of tendrils on the leaf stems, and need only a light support of string or wire.

***Lonicera* (Honeysuckle).** Either evergreen or deciduous (depending on how cold the winters are), these twining, rapidly growing vines can give you a dense mass of foliage in a very short time. Provide these plants with a frame and a few wires or strings and stand back! By the end of the growing season you'll have more privacy than you thought possible. Japanese honeysuckle *(L. japonica)* grows well in zones 5 through 10. The most commonly available variety is 'Halliana', whose fragrant white flowers appear in late spring. Trumpet honeysuckle *(L. sempervirens)*, suitable for zones 4 through 10, has scentless trumpet-shaped summer blossoms in yellow-orange to bright red; scarlet berrylike fruit follows in autumn.

***Rosa* (Rose).** As mentioned earlier, roses are not strictly vines, but the long canes of many varieties can be tied and trained to a fence or latticework to support their spectacular display of blossoms. Climbing roses are divided into two groups: ramblers and large-flowered climbers. Canes of the large-flowered climbers grow 10 to 15 feet tall and carry their flowers in clusters. There are also many tall-growing "sports" of hybrid tea roses and their descendants that match the foliage and bloom characteristics of their more shrubby ancestors. The foliage cover won't be very dense, but training the canes horizontally will encourage more blossoms.

Ramblers have 10 to 20-foot canes that bear clusters of small flowers. Their growth is rapid as long as they have some sort of support to lean on. They can take up quite a bit of space, but if you have the room, they'll provide you with a thick mass of foliage and a breathtaking display of blossoms during the growing season. Almost all roses are deciduous; their resistance to cold weather varies according to variety.

***Vitis* (Grape).** These deciduous vines can produce enough growth each year to provide shade and overhead privacy over a large pergola or arbor, provide a foliage extension on top of a wall or fence, or completely cover a wall. Grape is one of the few ornamental vines with dominant trunk and branch pattern for winter interest, bold-textured foliage, and colorful fruit. Most grape varieties grow moderately quickly; they will need to be trained and tied to their supports.

There are three classes of grapes: the European *(V. vinifera)*, the American *(V. labrusca)*, and wine grapes. Many different hybrid varieties exist among these main classes, with different hardiness tolerances and heat requirements to produce sweet fruit. Check with a local nursery to determine which varieties do best in your area.

Wisteria. Great beauty and vigor are the hallmarks of this deciduous vine, which does well in zones 4 through 10. Long, drooping flower clusters appear before the graceful foliage and long streamers of new growth emerge. Stems can twine around large supports, which should be heavy and sturdy enough to support the considerable weight of mature specimens. You can use wisteria along the top of a fence or wall to extend the height, across the top of an arbor for overhead privacy, or along a trellis to let the flowers and foliage drape a light screen.

STRIKING FLOWERS, FOLIAGE, AND FRUIT

Because of their fast growth rate, vines can be workhorse plants, but they can also be strikingly decorative. In the far left photo, *Clematis jackmanii* 'Rubra', supported by wires, wends its way across a brick wall. In the photo at near left, the foliage and fruit of a Cabernet Sauvignon grape orchestrate an autumn display.

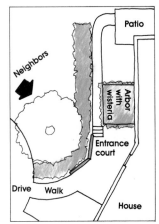

TRELLISES SEPARATE AND ENCLOSE OUTDOOR SPACES

A heavy trellis, supporting a venerable wisteria (photo at left) limits the view from an entry court to other parts of the garden as well as enclosing the space. A view of the entry court is shown on page 4. As the sketch above shows, the walk under the trellis leads to the more private, family oriented parts of the garden; the vine-covered trellis, helped by the change in levels, defines the transition from a "public" space to more private areas. Design: Thomas Church, San Francisco, CA.

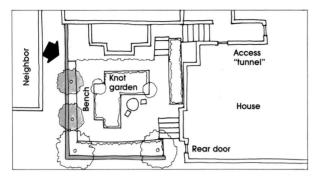

VINES TO CREATE A BARRIER

In the small (less than 25 feet square) back garden of landscape architect Thomas Church (sketch at left), ivy has been allowed to grow rampant over a wire fence to create a dense barrier (visible in the photos at middle left and bottom). The trellis over the neighbor's porch (bottom photo) is covered with white wisteria, which provides the definition of two distinct spaces.

On the plain board fence separating the front garden from the street, trunks of ivy have been trained in a diamond pattern.

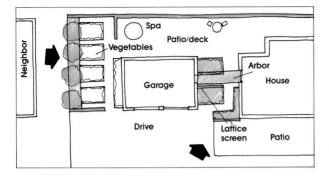

VINES TO CREATE PRIVACY, MASK FENCES

The front of the suburban home pictured on this page (sketch above) uses vines on a series of screens, trellises, and walls to create privacy and soften the lines of structures. The bottom photo shows the main entrance to the front door. A lath screen with a young wisteria protects the view of the entrance from the street.

A heavy-beamed trellis covered with primrose jasmine between the house and the garage provides a sense of enclosure, while another staggered screen being covered by Boston ivy screens the view of the deck beyond.

In the photo at right, the vegetable garden is protected by another lath screen with wisteria. Design by Jack Chandler, Yountville, CA

61

F E N C E S   A N D   S C R E E N S

Without a doubt, fences are the most common privacy barriers in gardens throughout the country. Their adaptability to a broad range of landscaping applications, the varied materials and styles available, and the relative ease and economy with which they can be built, all contribute to the popularity of fencing.

Because they are so easy to construct, fences are often the quickest way to solve your privacy problems. Shrubs and hedges would take months or even years to attain the height of a fence that can be put up in a weekend. Yet fences are much more than merely a "quick fix"; with a little planning and design, they can be a handsome, integral part of your garden landscape as well as providing the privacy you need.

In comparison with masonry walls, which are discussed in the next section, fences have some advantages and some disadvantages. On the positive side, fences are usually easier to construct and the materials less expensive to buy. The visual effect of fences is generally lighter and more adaptable to the style of the house. Also, fences can easily skirt or butt up against natural impediments along the line of the barrier, such as trees or boulders.

On the other hand, walls appear more imposing to intruders. Where noise is a consideration, walls provide a much more effective screen than fences. The additional initial expense of laying a masonry wall must be balanced against the fact that it will be essentially maintenance free, while most fences need regular maintenance to remain sturdy and attractive.

BUILDING TO CODE

Zoning ordinances have been mentioned before in regard to erecting barriers, and fences are no exception. You probably won't have to get a permit for a fence or wall lower than 3 feet, but it's a good idea to check with your local planning department anyway.

For fences or walls higher than 3 feet, you should definitely find out about any setbacks or other special requirements that must be met in your area. Local ordinances often specify the minimum setback from the street for a front fence, and a maximum height for front, side, and back fences.

FENCES ON THE BASE PLAN

Fences surround most of the perimeter of the sample plan except for the rear, where a masonry wall aids in noise control. An enclosure in the front of the house, complete with gates, provides a private outdoor area. The low picket fence along the sidewalk defines a semipublic space while still setting a boundary. A free-standing 8-foot screen and trellis shield a portion of the pool area, and a 5-foot chain-link fence protects small children from the pool.

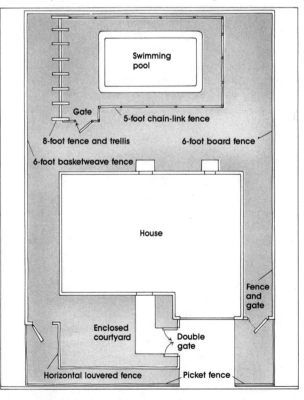

Opposite: The warm gray and richly textured surface of a redwood grapestake fence surrounding the small back yard of a townhouse in Virginia is enlivened by stripes of ivy that encircle a metal oriental ornament. Another view of this garden is shown on page 37.

Height restrictions often apply only to solid fences or walls; you may be able to exceed the maximum height if the top portion of your fence—or the whole thing—is open rather than solid. Or you may be able to obtain a variance to build the fence you want.

Building officials are usually pleased to help you with your project, and they can be of great assistance in helping you to prevent costly mistakes. Their job is to enforce the building code, the set of regulations that specifies the minimum standards for materials and workmanship. By constructing to these standards, you can be sure of the structural integrity of your fence.

PROPERTY LINES

If you plan to build a fence along your property boundary line, make doubly sure about the location of the line to prevent later disputes. Fences right on the property line are often planned, built, and maintained jointly by the two neighbors. If this arrangement will work for you, by all means take advantage of sharing the cost and effort of building and maintaining the fence. But if the fence is strictly your own initiative, place it about 6 inches in from the property line so that there can be no question about ownership and maintenance.

FENCES FOR PRIVACY

What do you think of when you hear the word "fence"? Perhaps an image of a charming picket fence, a sturdy board fence, or a durable chain link fence comes, to mind. The number of different designs and materials you can incorporate into any fence you build is practically limitless.

The terms "solid" and "open" describe different styles of fences that are used for different applications. As its name implies, a solid fence blocks the view completely, and limits the passage of light and air. An open fence has some openings that allow glimpses of the view from either side of the fence, and that allow light and air to pass through. A fence need not be either solid or open; it might be solid at the bottom and open at the top. The degree of openness varies from one fence style to another; a lattice fence allows some view beyond the fence, while a basketweave does not, although it does allow air circulation.

HOW LOW CAN YOU GO?

Don't rule out low fences from your consideration just because they will not completely block a view. By merely defining a boundary, you can often create a sense of enclosure that will make outdoor spaces more pleasant to use. A split-rail zig-zag fence, which is open and only 3 or 4 feet high, makes a charming backdrop for low plantings along the front of a yard. Add a rambling rose or two to trail along it and you'll have an attractive, effective barrier.

The height of the fence you need depends largely on the sort of activities that will be taking place behind it. If you're playing badminton on the back lawn, a 4-foot fence will not give you much privacy. But the same fence will give you all the seclusion you need if you're hunched over a chess board on a cozy side patio.

A low fence that does not provide the degree of privacy you wish can be augmented with a trellis. The extra height creates the feeling of separation of space, and with the addition of a trailing vine such as wisteria or a climbing rose, the sense of visual enclosure becomes complete.

SCREENS

Fences needn't be limited to the perimeter of your property. A *screen* is a fence that does not completely enclose an area. Freestanding fences, or screens, can be placed almost anywhere on your property. Screens are most often used as partial enclosures at the edges of specific areas, such as around a deck, on two sides of a swimming pool or hot tub, or along one edge of a lawn.

Screens can essentially be treated and designed in the same way as fences; but when you use them to define and enclose smaller areas, take care that they do not overwhelm the space they protect. Solid screens can effectively hide parts of your yard that are less than attractive. Compost heaps, garbage cans, dog runs, or potting areas can be easily shielded with a simple solid board fence.

If you decide to build a solid screen, be sure that it will not cast an unwelcome amount of shade on the area you are protecting or on adjacent plants. One solution to this problem is to use translucent fiberglass panels that will let the sun shine through, but still block unwanted views.

Latticework is particularly well suited to use as screens because it allows air to circulate and light to stream through. The criss-crossing of lath or other small-dimension lumber provides privacy and a sense of enclosure without a hemmed-in feeling.

DESIGNING YOUR FENCE

In thinking about the type and placement of fencing that will serve your need for privacy, it's helpful to refer to the plan you made of your property. The privacy rating you've given each area (see page 8) will also come in handy at this point, as you sketch potential locations for fences or screens.

For each fence or screen you sketched, think about any other functions that barrier might serve besides privacy. For example, a fence might also be designed to keep intruders out; to keep your own children or pets in and the neighbors' pets out; or to act as a windbreak. Listing these other functions will help you choose the right style of fence for your needs.

THE BASIC STRUCTURE

Most fences are constructed of three major elements: posts, rails, and siding. The posts are set in concrete, usually at intervals of 6 to 8 feet. Two rails run between the posts, one at the top of the posts, and one 6 to 8 inches above ground level. The rails tie together and brace the posts, as well as providing the structure to which the siding is nailed. Detailed instructions for constructing a fence can be found in the Sunset book *How to Plan & Build Fences & Gates.*

PUTTING YOUR BEST FENCE FORWARD

Most fences have a back and a front: the front is the side to which the siding is nailed, and the back shows the framework. For streetside fences, the front is positioned toward the street. Conventions concerning boundary fences with neighbors are often less clear. As a courtesy to your neighbors, you may wish to present the finished side to their view. In some communities, this courtesy is mandated by zoning regulations; in other localities the choice is left up to you.

You may wish to pick a fence design that presents the same appearance on both sides. For example, if the rails are channeled so that the siding slides into the middle of each set of rails, both you and your neighbor can enjoy a uniformly attractive appearance. Or you might alternate the panels of the fence so that between one set of posts the siding is nailed on one side, and for the next stretch it is nailed on the other. Thus each of you gets an equal share of the finished side and the frame side.

If you decide to give your neighbor the finished side of a fence (or if your neighbor has already presented you with the back of a fence), that doesn't necessarily mean that you are stuck with an unattractive view. If you want to dress up the back of your fence, you can add strips of lath in an interesting pattern; allow vines to cover the whole fence; hide it with shrubbery; or completely cover it with a lightweight bamboo or reed screen. A more expensive solution would be to add siding to match the front of the fence, or to match the siding of your house.

OPEN FENCES

The privacy ratings discussed earlier will be your starting point in determining the openness of your fence. Areas with high privacy ratings will require a more solid fence, but be careful to avoid an unfriendly fortresslike effect. Remember that it is often necessary only to break up the view—not obliterate it entirely—to create a sense of privacy.

There are varying degrees of "openness" and "solidness." You might have wide-open panels along the top of your fence, or a strip of criss-crossing lath. A louvered fence is an excellent style that allows some openness, while maximizing the amount of privacy provided. Placed horizontally, the louvers completely block the view from the outside. A somewhat more open effect results when they are installed vertically, allowing a succession of very narrow views of the yard inside to anyone interested in looking. You can use ¾-inch-thick slats with standard jalousie-window track to create adjustable louvers that can be solid or open as you wish.

The wind-chill factor. If you want your fence or screen to act as a windbreak, an open or partially open fence is more effective than a solid fence. Wind simply vaults over a solid fence and continues at the same velocity a few feet downwind from the fence. A wind screen or fence with an open design, on the other hand, breaks up a steady wind into a series of eddies or small breezes. Compared with the effect of a solid fence, the diffusing action of an open fence protects a larger area behind the fence or screen from the force of the wind.

NEIGHBORLY FENCE CONSTRUCTION

The basic elements of a fence are shown at left. Securely anchored posts give the fence its vertical stability; top and bottom rails provide horizontal stability and support the siding; and the siding itself provides the visual screen. Posts are generally 4 × 4's and rails 2 × 4's. The size of the siding varies with the style of the fence.

In order to construct a neighborly fence that presents the same appearance on both sides, siding can be inserted in the middle of the rails (right); or the siding in alternate panels between posts can be switched between one side and the other (center).

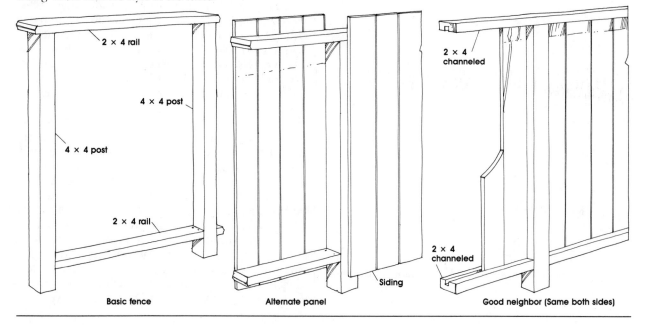

2 × 4 rail

4 × 4 post

4 × 4 post

2 × 4 rail

2 × 4 channeled

2 × 4 channeled

Siding

Basic fence

Alternate panel

Good neighbor (Same both sides)

Windows on the world. If you opt for a fairly solid fence style for reasons of privacy, but would like to preserve and enjoy certain views, you can plan windows in your outdoor room enclosure. This greatly relieves a hemmed-in feeling, and even the most mundane view becomes a bit more special when framed.

A panel of stained glass or frosted and etched glass can be set into a fence or screen to provide a focal point and expand the visual dimensions of the enclosure. Translucent plastic or fiberglass panels are inexpensive and, when set into a small fenced garden or deck, will bathe the area in sunlight.

SIDING STYLES

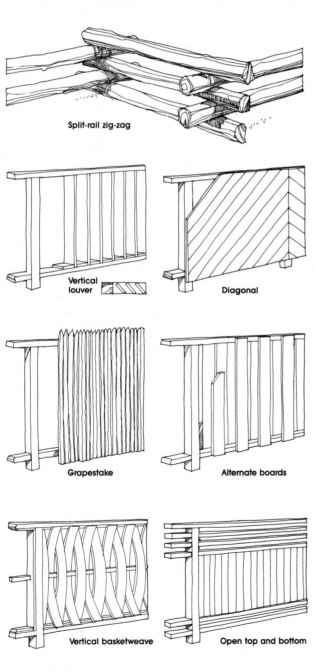

Split-rail zig-zag

Vertical louver

Diagonal

Grapestake

Alternate boards

Vertical basketweave

Open top and bottom

WIRE FENCES

Metal post and welded wire fences are easily installed by the homeowner who wants to fence a yard to keep children or pets in or out. Chain link fencing, which is better installed by professionals, provides a sturdy barrier that will deter all but the most determined intruder. Wire fences themselves will not provide you with very much privacy, but either type of fence can offer privacy when softened with plants. Shrubs can hide the starkness of the fence, and fast-growing vines such as ivy or honeysuckle can completely cover the fence in one or two growing seasons.

OTHER MATERIALS AND DESIGNS

The number of different kinds of fences you can build is limited only by the availability of materials in your area, and by your imagination. The following short list of other fencing materials and designs only suggests the wide range of possibilities.

Split-rail zig-zag. The design of this fence dates from pioneer times, when finished lumber was not readily available. It can add a rustic touch to any garden. Because these fences are very open and are ordinarily built no higher than 2½ to 3 feet, they will not give much privacy, but better serve as a boundary marker.

Basketweave. This fence is popular with do-it-yourselfers because it is easy to construct, allows air circulation even though it presents a solid barrier visually, requires a minimum of inexpensive materials, and has a pleasing interwoven design. The wood strips may be woven either horizontally or vertically. Because the strips are relatively thin to permit weaving, this fence is not particularly durable in harsh winter climates.

Grapestake or stockade. This siding is composed of thin stakes or poles nailed to the basic fence structure. In the West, redwood grapestakes are used to support grapevines in vineyards, and their rough-hewn texture complements almost any garden. East of the Rockies, stockade poles 2 to 3 inches in diameter are used to the same effect. The narrow verticals give a light effect without sacrificing privacy. They can also be used horizontally, or staggered for variety in appearance.

Shingles. Shingles are very easy to work with and provide a handsome appearance, whether painted or left to weather naturally. Shingles are a particularly good choice if the exterior of your house is also shingled.

Lattice. The criss-crossing of small pieces of wood gives lattice screens and fences a light, open effect. The openness of the fence is determined by the width of the space between the slats. Rambling vines can provide a counterpoint to the regular arrangement of the wood, as well as providing further privacy protection.

Reed or bamboo. Woven reed or bamboo screens can be stretched across a frame for a delicate effect that allows air circulation. These screens are a particularly good choice for gardens with an oriental theme or style. Lightweight bamboo and reeds are not a good choice for windbreaks or in areas with severe winters. They are relatively inexpensive, but even in mild-winter climates they will have to be replaced every two or three years.

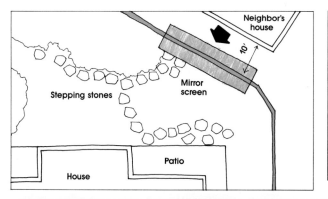

Stepping stones

Mirror screen

Neighbor's house

10'

Patio

House

IT'S ALL DONE WITH MIRRORS

The fence shown below does double-duty for the small yard it shields. A neighbor's house only 10 feet behind the fence is completely hidden from view; and the mirrors on the front of the fence make the small area that it shields seem much deeper than it actually is. The pot-ted ferns are rotated with other container plants during the year to create an ever-changing vista. The mirrors need periodic cleaning, but are other-wise maintenance-free. Design: Morris and White, San Antonio, TX.

FENCE STYLES TO FIT THE GARDEN STYLE

To avoid visual confusion and a messy look, keep the style of fences and screens in your garden as close as possible to the style of existing structures and garden features.

In the photo at the far left, a low bamboo fence encloses an oriental-style entrance landing, in coun-terpoint to the thick grove of its living cousins be-yond. Garden of Lois Brown, Pasadena, CA. In the photo at near left, a Victorian-style fence de-limits an area of the gar-den surmounted by the colorful clematis hybrid 'Lasurstern'.

AN UNOBTRUSIVE FENCE FOR FRONT YARD PRIVACY

The photos on this page and the sketch below show a suburban Seattle front yard that was transformed into a gracious entry court and sitting and dining area. The fence siding is clapboard to match the siding of the house.

Instead of carrying the solid siding a full 6 feet high, a gabled cap was constructed at the 5-foot level and a matching cap at the full height. The resulting gap gives the fence an airy feeling and makes the area it encloses less confining. In the photo above, the front door is to the right; the entrance gate (not visible) is to the left.

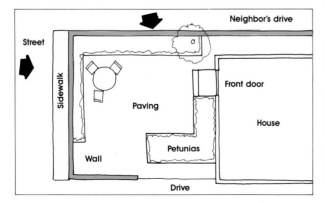

Neighbor's drive

Street

Sidewalk

Paving

Front door

House

Petunias

Wall

Drive

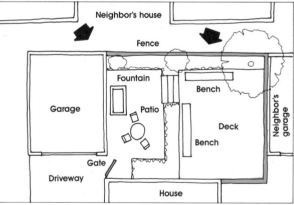

A TOTAL ENCLOSURE

The small back yard shown on this page is almost completely surrounded by close neighbors, particularly at the rear of the lot. A 4-foot poured concrete aggregate wall was constructed along the back of the lot, to which the fence was attached. This combination of wall and fence makes the actual height of the barrier less imposing. The fence is constructed of plywood panels with an overlay design of lath. The same lattice pattern is used against the wall of the garage behind the fountain (photo above), as well as on the deck against the neighbor's garage. Design: David Poot, Seattle, WA.

Walls have been a feature of garden design almost since building began. Houses, farms, and cities were surrounded by walls primarily as a defensive measure in early times; an extreme example is the Great Wall of China. This historic example of masonry was constructed in the second century B.C. along the 1500-mile border between the Chinese Empire and Mongolia. Although our needs for defense today are perhaps more subtle, solid masonry walls still provide a sturdy barrier against intrusions from the outside world.

Properly constructed, masonry walls will last for decades with little maintenance. Walls are the most effective barrier against noise. The warm colors of brick and natural stone complement the foliage of garden plants. You can create a unifying element in your garden design by using the same kind of stone in freestanding walls, retaining walls, paving, and the edging of raised beds.

Depending on your choice of materials, the cost of building a wall can be much greater than that of building a fence or screen or planting a hedge. Although the basic techniques are fairly simple, building a wall can be an overwhelming task if you do the work yourself. For walls 6 feet or higher, consultation with a structural engineer is highly recommended.

CHECKING CODES AND BOUNDARIES

As discussed in the section on fences (page 63), be sure to check out local codes and building requirements before you start construction of a wall. Walls are heavier structures and they require more expensive materials than most fences. You can prevent costly mistakes by adhering to the local codes.

If you intend to build a wall on or near the boundary line of your property, be sure you know exactly where the property lines are to forestall any disputes with your neighbors.

Opposite: This handsome wall curves gently to enclose a quiet entrance court. It is constructed of concrete, faced with roughly squared rubble stones, and topped by a brick cap. Design: Thomas Baak and Associates, Walnut Creek, CA; and Chris Casale, Casale Homes, Blackhawk, CA.

WALLS FOR PRIVACY

Walls can be as adaptable as fences in creating privacy in your landscape. Many people think of walls as massive, impenetrable structures; and although they can certainly be designed and constructed to achieve this effect, they do not necessarily have to be.

WALLS ON THE BASE PLAN

On the sample plan, a 3-foot natural stone wall skirts the front living space. This wall defines the area more than protects it, so groupings of shrubs could be planted to provide further visual protection. Brick walls shield the sides and present the neighbors with as attractive a view as you have. This consideration is less important at the rear, where the wall is constructed of economical concrete block.

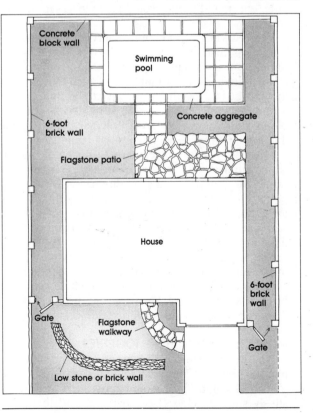

Concrete block wall

Swimming pool

Concrete aggregate

6-foot brick wall

Flagstone patio

House

6-foot brick wall

Gate

Flagstone walkway

Gate

Low stone or brick wall

A low stone wall at the front of the yard can mark your property line and enclose a small sitting area. If your front yard is large and underutilized, you can rearrange the grade. By excavating soil from one portion of the yard, you can create a small berm backed by a low (2 or 3 feet high) wall. The back of the wall is 3 to 4 feet high in the excavated area, effectively creating a sunken, protected outdoor living area.

Brick walls to create an entrance court can be designed with an open pattern of bricks that will let in light and air, but baffle the noise and view of passing traffic. If you're building a wall of concrete blocks, open decorative screen blocks can be added to lighten the effect.

Decorative screen blocks are an excellent choice for freestanding screens that can block views or separate parts of the garden without creating a hemmed-in feeling. Such a screen can block the view of the front door from the street, or give more privacy to a bedroom whose window is adjacent to the entry walk. A screen wall might hide and separate a potting area from the rest of the garden. Or two intersecting solid walls could provide a private space for sunbathing near the pool. If they have a southern exposure, the walls could also act as a heat trap to absorb the warmth of the sun during the day and radiate heat during cool evenings.

THE BUILDING BLOCKS

Building supply yards stock a number of types of materials suitable for wall construction. Your choice depends largely on the function and location of the wall, the general effect you want to achieve within the style already set by your house and garden, and how much time, effort, and money you plan to invest in its construction.

The "building blocks" of masonry construction are usually just that: regular units of clay or concrete whose dimensions are modular. That is, the three dimensions are simple divisions or multiples of each other so that they can be laid together in various configurations with a minimum of cutting to odd sizes. Brick, concrete block, and adobe block are all regular building units that lend themselves to wall construction.

Materials that are not regular units include concrete and natural stone. Concrete is a syrupy mixture of water, sand, gravel, and a binding agent that can be poured into almost any mold, or form, you may build for it. Natural stone usually comes in irregular shapes and sizes, which makes it time-consuming and demanding to lay.

You may also choose to combine different materials in the same wall. A poured concrete or concrete block wall, for example, could be covered with a veneer of brick or natural stone. Such walls go up much faster than if they were solid brick or solid stone.

MORTAR: HOLDING IT ALL TOGETHER

Except in a dry stone wall, mortar is used to bind the masonry together. Mortar is composed of cement, lime, sand, and water. Since mortar must be mixed in relatively small batches (large batches tend to harden before they're used up), masons usually mix the dry ingredients by the shovelful, and then add water. Packages of dry premixed mortar ingredients are available at building supply yards. Unless your job is very small, this is an unnecessarily expensive way to buy mortar.

Grout is mortar that is thin enough to pour. It is used to fill cavities in masonry walls and to secure vertical reinforcing rods. When grout sets up it locks a wall together into an essentially monolithic structure.

A FIRM FOOTING FOR YOUR WALL

Just as a house wall needs a firm anchor to the ground, so does a garden wall. As a rule of thumb, the width of the foundation, or footing, for a wall should be twice the width of the wall itself, with the wall centered above. The depth of the footing below ground level should be at least the width of the wall.

Poured concrete is the best material for footings. Forms for a footing are easy to build and, except for very long walls, the amount of concrete you need will be fairly small and easy to pour.

REINFORCING THE WALL

Any freestanding wall over 2 or 3 feet high should have some kind of reinforcement that ties portions of the wall together and prevents it from tipping over. Reinforcement can be accomplished either by steel bars built into the wall, or by pilasters at least every 12 feet along the wall. Before you proceed too far in your

PILASTERS FOR VERTICAL SUPPORT

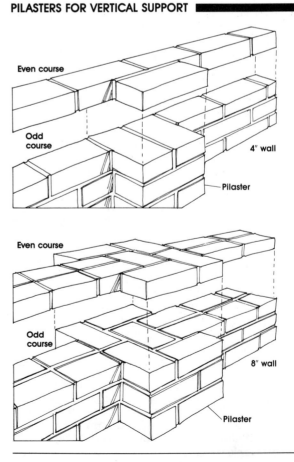

Even course

Odd course

4″ wall

Pilaster

Even course

Odd course

8″ wall

Pilaster

planning, check with your local building department to ascertain what they will require you to do.

Steel rods, or "rebar" (short for reinforcing bar), can provide either horizontal or vertical reinforcement. When laid with the mortar along the length of a wall, steel reinforcements help to tie different sections of a wall together. Placed vertically, as for example between double rows of brick or within the hollow core of concrete blocks, and secured by grout, rebar will add the vertical strength that keeps the wall from toppling of its own weight.

Pilasters are columns of masonry tied into the wall that provide extra vertical support. Pilasters are normally required every 12 feet to support each length of wall. Use pilasters also on either side of an entrance gate and at the ends of freestanding walls. Pilasters contribute visual interest that breaks up the monotony of a long stretch of wall. When you're planning the foundation of your wall, don't forget to take pilasters into account; the footing will have to be twice as wide as the pilaster.

A WIDE CHOICE OF MATERIALS

The following short descriptions of various masonry building materials will give you an idea of the various possibilities for building a wall for privacy and security. For further descriptions of styles and detailed instructions of the steps involved in designing and constructing a masonry wall, refer to the Sunset book *Basic Masonry Illustrated.*

BRICKS

For the beginning mason who has never built a wall, bricks are an excellent material to start with. They are easy to handle and place, and their uniform size makes planning the job simpler. The small size of bricks does mean that there will be more to lay than if you use, say, concrete blocks, but you'll soon establish a rhythm that makes the process enjoyable and even relaxing. One of Winston Churchill's preferred recreational activities was to lay brick walls at his country home as a means of escaping the pressures of wartime London.

Types of brick. Brick manufacturers provide the builder with a variety of colors, textures, and strengths from which to choose. Basically, bricks fall into two categories: common brick and the more expensive face bricks. Common bricks are less consistent in size, color, and texture than face bricks. Face bricks are manufactured of specially selected materials and are fired at a higher temperature than common bricks, which makes them stronger. Common brick is most often used for paving; face brick is preferable for freestanding walls.

Used bricks are sometimes available—usually at a premium price—from masonry yards. These bricks are salvaged from demolished buildings and walls, and are frequently marked, chipped, and stained with mortar. These "imperfections" will add texture and variety to your wall, imparting a slightly rustic look that will give the impression the wall has stood for a good deal longer than it actually has.

Sizes of brick. Most bricks are made in modular sizes— that is, the three dimensions are simple divisions of each other. The standard modular brick measures 8 inches long by 4 inches wide by 2⅔ inches high. This allows two headers (bricks running across the thickness of the wall), or three rowlocks (headers turned on edge), to equal the length of a stretcher (a brick running along the length of a wall). The actual dimensions of the bricks are somewhat less to allow for the standard ½-inch mortar joint.

Designing a brick wall. Brick walls can either run in a straight line or—because bricks are a small building unit—can be slightly curved. Angling each brick a little produces a slightly curving serpentine structure that is actually structurally stronger than a straight wall. Bricks can also be staggered to leave open spaces in the wall to allow for air circulation or give a more open screening effect.

Bond patterns. Throughout the 5,000 or so years that brick walls have been built, masons have developed patterns, or bonds, in which brick can be laid. These bonds are designed to give strength to the wall as well as to please the eye. The six most commonly used bonds are illustrated below. You can, of course, design your own bonding pattern, using the modular size of the bricks as your guide.

Before you settle on a bonding pattern, though, keep in mind how thick your wall must be and what kind of reinforcing, if any, will be required by local codes. Some bond patterns accommodate steel reinforcing more readily than others.

BONDING PATTERNS

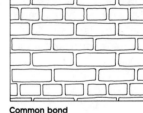

Running bond

Common bond

Flemish bond

English bond

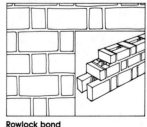

Stack bond

Rowlock bond

CONCRETE BLOCKS

The large size of concrete blocks makes construction of a wall gratifyingly rapid. The hollow core of the blocks makes it easy to add steel reinforcing and grout to construct an extremely strong wall. As if this were not enough, concrete block is one of the most inexpensive masonry materials you can buy.

Because it is inexpensive, concrete block has become linked in the minds of many people with "quick and dirty" construction projects lacking character and grace. But with a little imagination and planning, and judiciously choosing among the many types of blocks available, you can create an interesting and affordable wall in a short time. Or, if you prefer, you can use a concrete block wall as a core to be covered with a veneer of brick and natural stone.

Types of concrete block. Since masonry materials are usually produced regionally, the variety of blocks available in your area may vary somewhat from the choices outlined here.

Two weights of block are available. Standard blocks are molded from regular concrete aggregate, and weigh about 45 pounds each. Cinder blocks are made with a lighter-weight aggregate and weigh considerably less, although they are somewhat more expensive. Either type will work for garden wall, so you can make your selection on the basis of cost or of ease of construction.

Sizes of block. The large standard size of concrete blocks is 8 by 8 by 16 inches. There are usually a number of sizes that are fractional units of the standard size. Most blocks come in precise dimensions, which makes planning easy. Planning is essential, though, since the blocks are difficult to cut or split without a masonry saw.

Decorative block. Most manufacturers make a variety of decorative blocks that will give the surface of a wall more texture and interest. Sculptured-face blocks have patterns cast in relief on one side of the block. These blocks can be combined in various ways to produce an overall pattern.

Split-face blocks are actually broken apart in the manufacturing process, and their faces resemble cut stone. Using a variety of sizes in your pattern will make the resemblance to stone even stronger.

Slump blocks are pressed before they completely harden, which gives them an irregular appearance similar to cut stone. Due to the extra pressing, the overall dimensions of slump blocks vary somewhat.

Screen or grille blocks are designed to be laid on end. They form a patterned wall that admits light and air while still affording some privacy. Screen blocks can be used with regular blocks to allow openings in a wall, or by themselves as a decorative screening panel. They are not as strong as regular concrete blocks, and require extra horizontal and vertical reinforcement.

ADOBE BLOCKS

Adobe blocks are not as widely available as concrete blocks or brick, but if you do have a local source, adobe is certainly worth your consideration. Still a staple building material in the American Southwest, adobe is made from the claylike soil indigenous to the region. Asphalt stabilizers now make adobe blocks waterproof, and the rugged-looking earth-colored blocks harmonize well with all kinds of plantings. Adobe is best used in large, open gardens where the size of the blocks will be in scale; smaller gardens are likely to be overwhelmed.

Constructing with adobe. Adobe blocks are laid in a similar way to bricks and concrete blocks. For walls over 2 feet high, both horizontal and vertical reinforcement are necessary. Because of the weight of the adobe blocks, a strong foundation is imperative. The foundation should be built 6 inches above ground so that the blocks do not come in contact with the soil.

Finishing adobe walls. Adobe plaster covered with a coat of whitewash is the traditional finish for adobe. This gives a molded look to the completed wall, and was necessary to protect old-fashioned adobe from rain. But modern adobe requires no finish at all, and it's a good idea to postpone your decision on the finish until you've seen what the wall looks like in its setting. Once you plaster or paint the wall, its rustic appearance is lost. In any case, no maintenance is necessary.

NATURAL STONE

Natural stone walls are in keeping with any garden design or style, and are the top of the line when it comes to choosing a type of masonry. The cost of the stone itself, as well as the labor-intensive nature of laying natural stonework, makes this an expensive choice.

Stones can be laid either with or without mortar. You're limited in height with unmortared stone walls, however; freestanding walls over 2 feet high should be mortared for stability and resilience. Low, unmortared walls will serve to mark areas and boundaries, but are less useful in providing privacy.

Types of stonework. There are two broad classes of stonework: rubble and ashlar. Rubble is widely variable in shape and size, while ashlar is more precisely cut. Rubble stones are more widely available and less expensive. Between these two extremes you'll find "roughly squared" stones—such as cobblestones—that provide a measure of uniformity without being precisely cut.

Stones used for rubble masonry are often rounded and of irregular shapes and sizes. Because of their widely varying shapes and sizes, it's not possible to lay regular rows of stones as with bricks or blocks. The stones are fitted by paying attention to overlap bonding—stones overlapped so that the vertical joints are staggered—and to the arrangement of different sizes in a pleasing manner.

Fully trimmed ashlar stone can be almost as easy to lay as blocks or brick. The flat surfaces and limited range of sizes make regular patterns possible and require less mortar than for rubble stone walls. Regular patterns give a formal effect, while the visual impact of a more haphazard design is informal in nature.

MASONRY WALLS FOR COLOR AND TEXTURE

Masonry walls have a rich, solid look that will age well. At the far left, a wall built of used brick in an openwork pattern allows breezes to ventilate the yard, yet diffuses the view for privacy. (Design: Casale Homes, Blackhawk, CA.) At near left, a natural stone rubble wall is complimented by a tracery of English ivy.

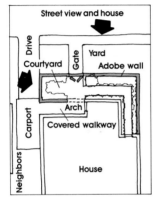

A PERFECT MELDING OF HOUSE STYLE AND PROTECTIVE WALLS

A secluded and secure entry court, photo at left, sketch above, was created by enclosing the area around the front door of a Spanish-style house with walls of stuccoed adobe. The result is a small intimate garden that introduces visitors to the special tranquility of the house. Antique Spanish Colonial doors protect the court from the street beyond. Design: Robert Fletcher, West Los Angeles, CA.

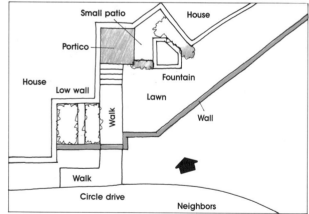

AN OASIS IN THE DESERT

The photos on this page and the sketch above depict the entrance court of a contemporary house in the southwestern United States. The photo at top shows the view through the entrance arch into the walled front garden. Desert plants are used outside the walls, while a luxurious green lawn entices the visitor into the courtyard. The photo at right, overlooking a welcoming fountain, shows the view from a small patio off the side of the house toward the entrance arch. Design: Steve Martino and Associates, Phoenix, AZ.

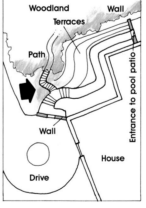

playful flair to the wall.
Design: Innocenti and
Webel, Long Island, NY.

BRICK WALL TO PROTECT A GARDEN

The brick wall shown in
the photo at top divides
the street from the garden.
The Flemish-bond-pat-
terned wall is built thicker
at the base; this results in
a constantly level line over
a variable grade, as well as
a secure foundation re-
quiring fewer pilasters
along the length of the
wall.

The openwork top of
the wooden gate carries
through the design motif
of the alternating bricks.
Design: David Campbell,
VA..

BRICK PATTERNS FOR A POST-MODERNIST EFFECT

The brick wall (photo at
left, sketch above)
shielding this back yard
uses the same English
bonding pattern as the
brick of the house, but incorporates additional surface indentations in a symmetrical design to add a

G A R D E N   S T R U C T U R E S

A garden filled with trees, shrubs, flowers, and lawns may be delightful to look at, or to stroll through, but it needs something more if it is actually going to be lived in. Edith Wharton, the American writer who lived much of her life in Europe, noted after visiting many Italian villas and gardens that "the grounds were as carefully and conveniently planned as the house," and that "the old Italian garden was meant to be lived in— a use to which, at least in America, the modern garden is seldom put."

Among the most dependable resources for attaining the essential atmosphere of privacy in your garden are covered garden structures—structures that lend the garden a special sense of seclusion that invites you to live there, not merely to look at it from indoors or to walk through it now and then.

Arbors, trellises, gazebos, and the like are types of garden architecture that seem to have fallen out of popularity in recent years. Yet their function in the garden is an important one, and deserves a second look, especially in terms of the privacy they can provide.

EXTENSIONS OF THE HOUSE

Some of the most convenient and serviceable covered structures are close to home: They extend the house into the garden, acting as a transitional area between the two, and may include such facilities as a hot tub, spa, or dining area. They are usually more protected from sun and wind, and in some cases temperature extremes and precipitation, than are detached structures.

GARDEN ROOMS

Whatever it's called—lanai, enclosed porch, or covered patio—a garden room can meet your needs for private

Opposite: Portions of this second-story roof deck are protected from Seattle's heavy rain and from the gaze of third-story neighbors by a wooden trellis surmounted by translucent fiberglass. The outdoor rooms greatly extend the interior living spaces. Another view of the deck can be found on page 35. Design: David Poot, Seattle, WA.

and sheltered outdoor living next to the house. Its solid roof provides protection from the elements, and its walls and floor make it a year-round habitat for plants and people. If you live in a cold-winter area, you can enjoy your garden room by insulating it with thermal glass.

PORCHES

This traditional outdoor room has a solid roof but no other walls. It may be entirely open or partially screened by vine-covered trellises. In regions where mosquitoes, flies, and gnats are a nuisance, open walls can be constructed with window screening to keep insects out without sacrificing ventilation. Retractable wooden, bamboo, reed, or canvas shades can provide adjustable vertical screening to block sunlight and increase privacy.

OVERHEADS

Any type of rooflike structure—solid, open, or partially filled in—may be attached to the house to create or enhance privacy, make shade, or provide shelter from wind and rain. A fast-growing vine will soften the effect of the overhead and increase privacy and shade.

A structure that is open overhead will offer ventilation on a hot summer day, while a solid overhead will protect you from precipitation during the winter. If you decide on a solid overhead, be sure to allow a slope of ¼ inch per foot of roof so that rain and melting snow can drain away.

Although most outdoor ceilings are fixed permanently in position, a movable ceiling can be a great convenience. You can install sliding or folding panels of wood, bamboo, canvas, or other material for easy adjustment to provide the amount of sun, shade, ventilation, or privacy you wish.

The simplest type of overhead is a trellis extending the rafters of the roof, affording some overhead privacy and shade, but mainly fostering a sense of shelter and seclusion. If your trellis is meant to support vines, don't go to a great deal of effort to construct an elaborate or complicated design. Most vines are fast-growing, and will virtually obliterate your handiwork in a season or two.

LATH OVERHEADS

Lath overheads are simple to design and easy to build. Varying the space between the strips produces different patterns of light and shade.

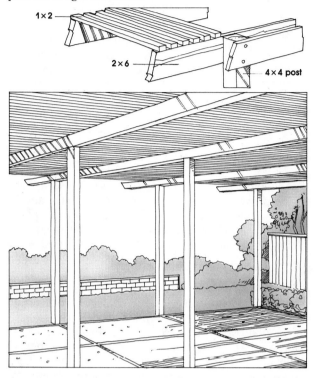

EGGCRATE OVERHEADS

The addition of vines or translucent panels on top of eggcrate overheads provides complete privacy; or leave the structure open to the sky.

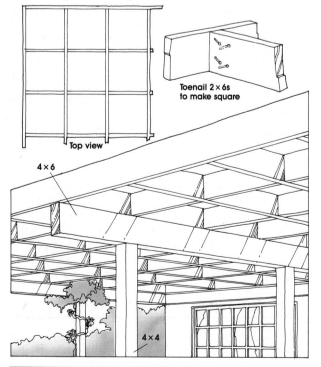

The most popular use of an overhead structure is to cover a patio or deck adjacent to the house. You can use 4-by-4 posts and beams, and rafters of whatever size you prefer, to make a substantial open cover. The direction and spacing of the rafters control sunlight as well as privacy from particular vantage points. A number of coverings can be used with such a framework, or with steel supports. Lath is a favorite material for enclosing semisheltered structures for plants; it also makes shade, and some privacy, while still permitting the free circulation of air. Bamboo and reeds make an attractive, natural-looking, but not very durable overhead covering; they admit less light and allow less air circulation than lath. Prefabricated panels of lattice can be installed easily, and just as easily removed according to the dictates of the seasons. Annual vines make removable latticework less open; permanent latticework can be covered with perennial vines.

Several types of solid material admit varying amounts of light while blocking air circulation, an advantage in windy spots but a disadvantage in hot ones. Fiberglass panels are quite durable. Different types of fiberglass vary considerably in the amount of light they admit. Canvas is one of the most attractive overhead covers, and can be easily attached to most kinds of framework.

COVERED WALKWAYS

Pergolas, some arbors, and covered breezeways fall into this category. These structures often play the important role of linking two separate parts of the garden together—the patio and the vegetable garden, for example. Aside from offering some shelter for those who pass through them, covered walkways are the perfect support for vines such as wisteria, climbing roses, clematis, or grapes. The addition of a bench or two can turn a vine-covered walkway into an enticing spot to stop and rest a moment.

BREEZEWAYS

Linking the house to the garage or to a utility or work structure, a breezeway offers solid overhead protection. Structurally and architecturally, it is usually a continuation of the house, built of the same materials, painted the same color. If it is very long, it requires posts or columns for support.

PERGOLAS

Because it is more open and usually more decorative, and because it is often detached from the house, a pergola has greater potential than a breezeway as a distinctive architectural element in the garden. A pergola is an enclosure linking one part of the garden with another or just providing a shaded, private cover, with or without seats, for a section of walkway. Constructed of sturdy columns, pillars, or rustic logs with beams and rafters, a pergola is nearly always wide enough to allow two people to walk side by side. Because pergolas are substantial structures, their construction is sometimes governed by building codes. You may use vines to enhance a pergola's beauty and to increase shade and privacy.

GARDEN HOUSES

Arbors, bowers, gazebos, poolside shelters, teahouses, and pavilions fall into the "houselike" category because they all have at least a semblance of floor, ceiling, and walls. Dating back many centuries in England, garden houses were once referred to as "shadow houses." Because they stand separate, often across the garden from the house, these structures provide not only shade and privacy, but a special sense of seclusion in a romantic setting. Variations on this basic idea have decorated gardens and provided shelter and privacy through the ages.

Modern garden houses frequently adapt old forms to new uses, so that spas and pool facilities, for example, can be enclosed or flanked by useful, attractive garden structures. The design of any of these structures should be compatible with the character of the home that shares its setting. Although a garden structure need not be in the same style as the house, it should be planned with comparable scale, proportion, and material in mind.

A freestanding shelter may have the fantasy look of a Victorian gazebo or the rustic feel of an English cottage, or it may echo the subtle proportions and wood tones of a Japanese teahouse. Whatever its style, the shelter should rest comfortably in its setting. As a focal point, such a structure not only provides privacy and shelter, it attracts the visitor to explore and enjoy the garden.

ARBORS

Taking its name from the Latin word for tree, an *arbor* is a simple garden shelter that provides support for vines. The vertical supports may be evenly spaced metal pieces, wood, or even tree trunks. Its floor plan is usually rectangular. Visually, the most important aspect of an arbor is the vine that covers it, not the details of the support itself. Its Latin name indicates its intended function: to give the kind of shelter that a tree might provide. It is the simplest of garden structures.

The walls of an arbor can be any sort of crosshatching that supports vines, and the roof can be the same material. In many arbors, the walls curve inward to form the roof. The floor can be a solid platform.

An arbor should be constructed of sturdy, durable materials. When the framework of an arbor decays, its covering vines have to be removed before the arbor can be repaired. Periodic repair of the arbor poses no problem if it is covered with annual or very fast-growing vines.

BOWERS

In its traditional form, a *bower* is a garden shelter formed by vines or the boughs of trees twined together. The distinction between a bower and an arbor has become blurred; but a true bower has more the shape of a simple house, sometimes with a peaked roof, and is used as a cool place to sit. A bower may include either built-in seating, or movable benches or chairs.

A FRAGRANT BOWER

As well as being one of the most charming garden structures to look at, a small bower provides a secluded spot to sit and chat or read. It can be designed as a focal point at the end of a path, or as a walk-through structure marking the transition from one part of the garden to another. Fragrant-flowering vines add a further dimension. Avoid rampant vines; they can tear apart a lightweight structure and smother architectural details.

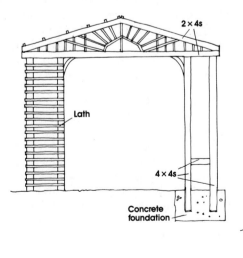

2 × 4s

Lath

4 × 4s

Concrete foundation

STRUCTURES OF VARYING COMPLEXITY

A series of simple archways to display vines and accentuate a pathway.

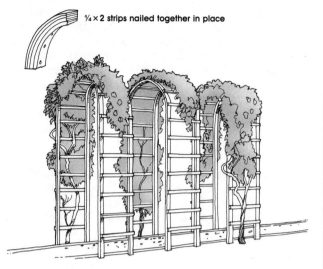

¼ × 2 strips nailed together in place

Gazebos are more complicated to construct, but many styles come in kit form.

Major poolside structures usually require the help of an architect and perhaps a contractor.

GAZEBOS

Gazebos originated in medieval times, as watchtowers atop fortress walls—a far cry from their more recent function as peaceful and fanciful structures for the garden. In Victorian times, gazebos were elaborate and ornate; some were fashioned of wrought iron. A modern gazebo may be of any architectural style that suits a garden setting. The traditional gazebo has a solid roof. However, you might decide to create a structure that functions like a traditional gazebo but has an open grid, with or without vines, for a roof. Most gazebos have floors, and some have built-in seating. Usually gazebo walls are open above seating level so that visitors can sit and look at the garden. Below seating level, trelliswork or sturdier cross-hatching, with or without vines, provides a sense of enclosure.

A *belvedere* is essentially a gazebo situated on high ground for a beautiful view of the garden. It is usually a permanent structure of a definite architectural style.

LOGGIAS

A *loggia* is a large rectangular outdoor sitting room, enclosed on one of the long sides and covered by a solid roof. Usually set at the edge of a garden, it offers loungers a sweeping view back across the grounds. Often of classical design, with pillars and formal symmetry, a loggia usually mirrors the architecture of the house and is meant to be seen for itself, not hidden with vines. Loggias are most appropriate to large gardens and estates, but more modest versions, usually referred to as *pavilions* or *cabañas*, often look onto swimming pools, lawns, or flower beds.

TRELLISES

Not in itself an enclosure but often used for the walls and roof of garden structures, a *trellis* is latticework made of strips of wood nailed together or to frames to form a grid. The most common construction material is 1¼-inch lath, but heavy dowels or other forms of wood may also be used. The grid may be a simple horizontal and vertical pattern, or a diamond pattern, or simply horizontal strips between upright posts. Its function is often to support vines as well as to form vertical walls. Trellises should be constructed of durable wood or treated with a preservative, and should be heavy enough to support for many years the kind of vines you intend to plant.

SPA AND POOLSIDE STRUCTURES

Hot tubs, spas, and pools all have special privacy requirements if they are to be enjoyed fully. Any of the freestanding "houselike" structures described above, when placed next to a pool or spa, will add a degree of screening and privacy, but you may have additional needs. If your hot tub or pool is located away from the house, you may want to have some type of changing room nearby, perhaps combining an arbor, dressing room, and storage for pool maintenance equipment all in one structure. With the addition of a pavilion or a vine-covered arbor, such a structure also screens the neighbors' view from the side and overhead.

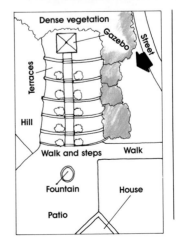

SOMETIMES YOU WANT PRIVACY FROM YOUR OWN HOUSE

The simple square garden house with an oriental flavor, shown in the photo above, provides a focus to the series of stairs leading up through the terraced hillside garden (sketch at left). The structure—technically a *belvedere* because of its elevated site—also acts as an enticement to explore the garden by providing a destination for strollers. Or it can be used as a private retreat, a place to curl up with a good book away from interruptions and distractions.

The retaining walls are angled toward the steps, rather than perpendicular to them, which gives the illusion of larger planting beds. Design: Thomas Church, San Francisco, CA.

A FANCIFUL STRUCTURE INVITES CONTEMPLATION

Garden structures can act as decorative elements in the garden all year round. Above top, a fanciful gazebo built on a platform at the edge of a pond in Pennsylvania provides a cheery note to a woodland garden bursting with daffodils and budding trees. Design: Renny Reynolds, Bucks County, PA. Directly above, a bench incorporated into a fence invites repose in a summer garden.

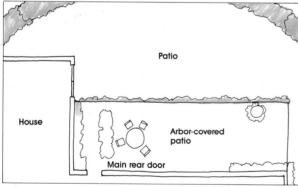

OVERHEAD SHELTER

A heavy-timbered over-head, shown in the top photo, shelters a terrace that is much used during the warm months of the year. Tucked into an "L" of the house (see the sketch, above), the space is further sheltered by hanging baskets of ferns, alyssum, and ivy. Design: Thomas Church, San Francisco, CA.

A FRAGRANT RETREAT

A corner of a roof deck in San Francisco, at right, offers an inviting spot for reading or contemplation. Surrounded by fragrant vines of jasmine and honeysuckle, as well as lemon blossoms and petunias, the small space provides a welcome retreat.

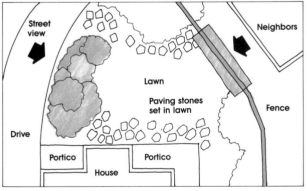

A GENEROUS UPDATE OF THE OLD-FASHIONED PORCH

The top photo shows a portion of the porch that surrounds the front of a contemporary guest house (sketch above). The expansive effect was achieved by extending the eaves of the house a generous distance from the house itself. The ceramic tile floor surface provides a visual transition from house to garden, as well as being easily maintained. Recessed overhead lighting makes the space usable on warm evenings. Another view of the privacy screen at right can be found on page 67. Design: Morris and White, San Antonio, TX.

UPHILL NEIGHBORS CAN'T SEE INTO LATH HOUSE RETREAT

The lathhouse in the photo above was added to the back of the house to ensure privacy from close neighbors higher up the hill. It also provides a shady spot for dining or lounging on hot summer days. A circular cutout allows a view of the garden. Design: Thomas Baak and Associates, Walnut Creek, CA.

Enhancements—the little niceties that make a garden special—are of particular importance in a landscape planned for privacy. A fountain, a statue, or lights to make the area accessible at night make a garden a unique expression of your own personality. Such personal touches make the garden seem more intimate, strengthening the sense of privacy and retreat.

Although they are often last on the list of things to add to a garden, it would be a mistake to see these enhancements as mere "extras." It's the little something special that makes a garden memorable.

This section offers ideas and information about fountains and pools; lighting in the garden; garden furniture; ways of attracting birds; statues and pottery; and a sampling of finishing details to make your garden more attractive and more livable.

WATER

Perhaps more than any other enhancement, water adds both life and serenity to the garden. In movement or in repose, water soothes the spirit. The very presence of water in the garden seems to lighten the oppressiveness of a hot day. In terms of privacy, though, it's the *sound* of water—its ability to mask background noises—that's important. The rhythmic sounds of moving water—bubbling, splashing, trickling—are as relaxing as birdsong or wind in a pine tree.

POOLS

A small stone or concrete basin or a wooden half-barrel, adorned with a few water plants, can create as strong an effect as a large pool. In an informal garden you might sink a miniature pool among ferns and a few rocks to brighten a shady corner. In a formal garden, position the pool along the central axis, either midway or at the end of the garden. For an oriental feeling, nestle a large stoneware bowl among pebbles,

Opposite: A small poured-concrete pool, inspired by natural granite pools found in California's Sierra Nevada, catches the interplay of light and a reflected tree fern in a hillside garden. Design: Harland Hand, El Cerrito, CA.

a fine-textured ground cover like baby's tears, and a clump of mondo grass. Accent the arrangement with a small stone lantern that doesn't overpower the pool.

Consider a small shallow reflecting pool set in front of or beneath an especially graceful shrub, small tree, or clump of showy flowers. Reflection amplifies the beauty of the special feature and adds dimension and life to a small space.

In a formal garden, a simple geometric shape is most appropriate for a pool. In an informal garden, either a geometric shape or a free-form design can work well. Brick, cut stone, concrete, molded plastic or fiberglass, vinyl sheeting shaped in a bed of sand, and concrete blocks are commonly used materials. Trim can help to tie the pool into the architectural style of your house and garden: for example, tiles for a Mediterranean or Spanish-American style house; treated wood or smooth concrete, simple and unadorned, for a contemporary style; brick or smooth-cut stone for a traditional American style.

Especially if your pool is in full sunlight, you can expect algae to develop. In sun or shade, mosquitoes breed in still water. A recirculating pump with a filter, and the addition of goldfish or koi, water snails, and water plants will control these problems. In even the smallest pools, mosquito fish thrive on mosquito larvae. Pools require occasional cleaning and repair, so if your pool is too large to be siphoned or ladled dry, it will need an efficient drain system.

WATERWORKS

By itself, a fountain means little in terms of privacy. But in a garden setting it can be a powerful means of achieving that rare form of privacy known as serenity. Close up, the sound of falling water is very effective in screening neighboring noises; the water doesn't so much drown out the sounds as focus the attention on something pleasant and close at hand.

Like pools, fountains can be large or small, formal or informal. Ready-made concrete and aggregate fountains are widely available. Quality of design and finish varies considerably, so be sure to shop around. Or instead of buying a ready-made fountain, you can incorporate a fountain into any pool, no matter how small

Recirculating water trickling from a bamboo spout has a soothing effect in an oriental-style garden.

A more elaborate undertaking for a larger garden—a tiled pool with a fountain and seating around the edge.

it is: recirculating pumps in a wide range of sizes, in conjunction with specialized nozzles, can create a gentle bubbling, a jet, a spray, a steady trickle, or a smooth, even flow of water.

A wall fountain can lend special charm to a small formal garden, and enhance a bare expanse of wall. A pump recirculates the water that spills from a wall-mounted spout into a basin or narrow pool below. For extra elegance, you might fashion a small alcove for the fountain and add trellised vines or espaliers to the wall.

If you decide on a water feature that uses a recirculating pump, look for a submersible pump made specifically for this purpose and sold at many nurseries and garden supply stores. Pumps range in capacity from a 1/55-horsepower model that lifts 135 gallons of water an hour to a height of 2 feet, to one that lifts 675 gallons an hour to a height of 12 feet. The pump sits unattached on the bottom of the reservoir and requires only the simplest plumbing: flexible plastic tubing carries water to the fountainhead. Once the reservoir is filled, you need to add only enough water to compensate for what is lost by evaporation and splashing.

If your water supply and drainage system permit, even without a recirculating pump you can still make a modest fountain with a steady drip or trickle—for example, a bamboo drip tube above an earthenware Japanese bowl surrounded by plants that enjoy moisture. From a naturalistic stone bank planted with mosses and ferns, you might devise a drip or seep that appears to be a natural spring.

LIGHTING

Aside from its obvious practical functions of security; safety around stairs, paths, and changing garden levels; and opening the garden to nighttime use, lighting used skillfully is a basic means of enhancing your garden's aura of seclusion and sanctuary. With garden lighting you can illuminate whole areas or accent attractive features such as flowering plants, strong-textured foliage, statuary, or architectural details. At the same time your garden is visually isolated from the dark world outside, intensifying the feeling of a private world. Lighting also enables you to enjoy the scene from in-

doors in any weather or season—what could be more striking than a softly illuminated, snow-covered garden?

KINDS OF LIGHTING

Much outdoor lighting is done with spotlights and floodlights. Try to conceal the lights themselves, under the eaves of the house or behind trees and shrubs. To avoid attracting insects, keep these bright lights away from sitting and dining areas.

Garden areas and low features are often lighted from above, and downlighting has the advantage of suggesting sunlight or moonlight. Wherever you use it, however, be sure that it doesn't cast harsh shadows and that it is positioned so that strollers in the garden don't pass through its beams.

Lighting from below can bring out the forms and textures of higher features, such as the deeply-cut bark and heavy, sprawling branches of an old oak. Position lights out of sight, either above eye level or directed away from the vantage points of people in the garden.

Backlighting to show off the silhouette of a feature with an interesting profile, like a small, contorted tree or a gracefully proportioned stone lantern, can create an extremely dramatic nighttime effect.

Statues, specimen plants, and other special features can be spotlighted from whatever angle you prefer. Many garden ornaments are best lighted from more than one angle, as long as the lights don't shine into the eyes of viewers.

Diffused lighting makes use of a translucent material like fiberglass or frosted glass, overhead, in a wall panel, or in a lantern, to create a soft, nonglaring light. Much the same effect can be achieved by indirect lighting, created by shining light onto a reflective surface such as a solid overhead.

A little experimentation will reveal which special lighting effects work best in your garden. Underwater lights in a swimming pool or ornamental pool cast a soft glow, and sparkle when the water's surface is disturbed. Japanese paper lanterns suspended in trees or beneath low eaves or overheads give a soft light and create a festive ambience. Garden torches, which burn scentless kerosene or alcohol, have the appeal of a

A niche or opening in a masonry wall is the perfect spot to show off a statue or colorful potted plants.

flickering fire and evoke a tropical atmosphere. Light from an outdoor fireplace or firepit is both dramatic and comfortable, when supplemented by soft indirect electric lighting to make the area bright enough to move around in.

PLANNING AND INSTALLATION

Whether you decide to install your garden lighting yourself or to call in professional help, allow sufficient time for experimentation to determine which kinds of lighting you will use, and where. It's difficult to anticipate the most pleasing placement of lights in the garden; so try moving one or more spotlights with bulbs of various wattages around the garden, and devise movable lamps and other kinds of temporary lights, before you choose permanent lighting. That way you can be certain that every light is placed effectively, and that it contributes to your garden's atmosphere of privacy.

Low-voltage systems make outdoor lighting safer and less expensive to use than regular 120-volt wiring, and also make it easier for you to do your own installation. You will need a transformer to reduce your 120-volt household current to 12-volt current. Most modern garden light transformers simply plug into any properly installed outdoor outlet. From the transformer, the 12-volt wiring can be buried a few inches deep, strung along fencing, or run up tree trunks. Even if you hire an electrician to do the installation, the cost will be considerably less than the cost of installing 120-volt lighting. Because the system is so flexible and no special conduits are needed, you can easily adjust or move low-voltage fixtures as your needs or ideas change, or as your plants grow.

FURNITURE

Like pools and fountains, garden furniture is not, in itself, a means to gaining privacy; but it certainly plays an important supporting role.

The uses that you make of your outdoor rooms will determine what kind of furniture you'll need. Seats of course are the most basic necessity. You'll also want tables to accommodate dining, writing, or game playing, as well as incidental tables, especially in sitting areas, that function like indoor coffee tables. If you

enjoy sunbathing, you'll want one or more chaises longues or deck chairs.

Umbrellas, especially large ones, can be used as movable overhead protection—both from the elements and from neighboring views. An umbrella adds a festive touch to the garden, making any outdoor event seem like a celebration.

Garden furniture should be sturdy and weather resistant. You may prefer built-in furniture for esthetic and practical reasons, or permanent furniture for its solidity and sculptured effect, or light furniture for ease of shifting and flexibility of arrangement.

BUILT-IN FURNITURE

Furniture that is built into the garden as an immovable feature has the advantage of blending exactly with the overall design so that it never looks cluttered or out of place. Built-in furniture is usually made of smooth stone, concrete, or weather-resistant wood. Benches are often incorporated into the inner walls of a gazebo or a pergola. Around a fire pit, they help to create the coziness of a campfire setting, but with greater comfort and a stronger sense of enclosure.

Built-in seating can also save space. The cap of a retaining wall at the edge of a flower bed or around a tree can be designed extra-wide to double as a bench or a bench-table. Cushions can be stored nearby for use whenever such a seat is used for longer than a few moments.

PERMANENT FURNITURE

Permanent garden furniture isn't usually fixed in place, but its weight and massiveness mean that it can't be moved about casually. A common example is the picnic table with attached bench seats, serviceable for writing, games, and other sedentary pastimes as well as dining. Wrought-iron benches, chairs, and tables are also substantial enough to give an air of substance and permanence. English gardens often feature heavy teak benches of Chinese Chippendale design, simple wooden platform benches, or semicircular, white-painted, high-backed benches. These seats are positioned along walks, in bowers or garden houses, or near a special feature such as a pool, fountain, or statue, where they invite the passerby to a moment's repose and contemplation.

MOVABLE FURNITURE

Seats and tables that can be lifted, slid, or rolled from one place to another have the particular advantage of ease and flexibility of arrangement. To the traditional repertoire of canvas chairs, chaises longues, and tables has been added a wide variety of sturdy, weather-proof, tubular metal furniture with metal, plastic, or treated cloth seating surfaces, including cushions that withstand the elements. Aluminum-and-vinyl chaises longues for sunbathing are light enough to move with one hand as you follow the sun about the garden. The lightness and durability of this kind of furniture, and in many cases its superior design, make it a desirable enhancement for any garden designed to be lived in.

AMENITIES FOR THE BIRDS

Into every garden visited by birds come music, color, life and movement, and something of untamed nature. What other combination of elements could so effectively transform even the plainest garden space into an intimate world apart? Observing birds through a season, a day, or even a random hour can be an absorbing and renewing experience.

WATER AND FOOD

The pools and fountains discussed earlier are excellent sources of drinking and bathing water for birds, which are quick to discover and use these garden features. In fact, a birdbath can double as a water feature and as an architectural sculpturelike ornament in your garden. If you devise a birdbath, be sure that the edges slope gradually and are textured to provide sure footing for birds. Wash the birdbath out frequently, and keep the water fresh. In winter, an immersion heater designed to function in no more than 3 inches of water will provide water when elsewhere there's only ice.

Trees and shrubs laden with fruit and berries will attract many birds, but bird feeders maintained all year round will attract more birds of more kinds. For most birds, a suitable diet includes commercial seed and grain mixes and, in winter, a supplement of suet or other form of fat. In winter you should also set out grit or coarse sand. Table scraps, bits of baked goods, peanut butter, fruits and dried fruits like raisins, and nuts are appreciated by various kinds of birds. Situate feeders (and birdbaths too) where they are secure from cats and other predators, and where rain and snow won't touch the food. Different kinds of birds feed at different heights from the ground, so position your various feeders to suit the local birds.

NESTING PLACES

Birds may be slow to recognize your hospitality, but it's likely that proper nesting places will eventually be used. Because birds are territorial, you will probably attract only one pair of a species; but if you provide appropriate and safe nesting sites, you may attract pairs of several different species.

You can buy birdhouses and nesting shelves, or build them yourself. Attach houses and nesting shelves securely in place, positioned so that openings are sheltered from prevailing wind and rain, and so that they are safe from predators. You can encourage birds to nest by placing nest-building or lining materials like short bits of string, shredded absorbent cotton, and loose bundles of twigs in places off the ground where birds will find them.

ORNAMENTS AND OTHER DETAILS

Pools, fountains, beautifully lighted paths, and wooden benches, if chosen with care and sensitivity to the overall garden design, are ornaments. They enhance the beauty as well as the peaceful ambience of the secluded garden. But they are functional and utilitarian as well as ornamental. One or a few well-chosen pieces of art may be what's needed to complete your sanctuary.

STATUES AND POTTERY

Historically, statuary and ornamental pots and urns have provided focal points in gardens all over the world. In formally laid-out western gardens they are often positioned in the center or at the end of a garden "room"—places to which the eye is led by the overall design of the space. A handsome sundial or a classically proportioned and styled urn or large pot is frequently used instead of a statue.

An elaborate, ornate statue depicting a classical subject is out of place in an informal garden—and often in a formal one as well. One simple, unpretentious piece, in correct proportion to the size of your garden space, can provide you with enjoyment that deepens as you live with it. A second piece in the same space, however, often creates an impression of clutter.

PEEPHOLES

Nothing else enhances the feeling of privacy in a garden in quite the same way as a peephole into the world beyond, or into another part of your garden. Of course, you don't want to create a random gap in a wall facing your neighbor's garage or a busy intersection; but an artfully contrived peephole can sometimes be devised to reveal a beautiful or interesting view, and to make you feel all the more secluded behind your wall, fence, or hedge.

You're fortunate indeed if you enjoy a view from your property of a natural feature—a distant mountain or bay, a canyon side, a magnificent maple, or even a neighbor's perfect lawn. Often, though, such a vista is flanked by a telephone pole bristling with wires, or by a huge neon sign. In that case, you can design your fence, hedge, or wall with a "window" that frames the view but conceals the ugliness and still keeps your garden private. Old glazed Chinese tiles (or reproductions) can be set in the wall or fence to frame the view.

If two outdoor rooms in your garden are divided by a hedge or other barrier and linked by a gate, consider using an open-grillwork gate that frames the view beyond, and place a focal feature—perhaps a pond with water plants—in line with the approach to the gate. The space on both sides of the gate is made more special by the glimpse of what lies beyond.

THE SMALLEST DETAIL

The smallest details have a special way of enhancing your garden. A handpainted address on a Mediterranean-style stucco fence; an antique ornamental grill as a "peek-through" in a solid garden gate; a niche in a stucco wall for an ornamental pot or small sculpture; or colorful flags to announce a festive occasion can make the difference between an attractive garden and an unforgettable one. When it comes down to this level of detail your garden makes an intensely personal statement, saying "this is mine," "this is me." That's what makes gardens, and the privacy they provide, so wonderful: they're the perfect place to freely create a reflection of yourself while working with nature to create a more beautiful world.

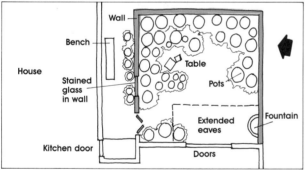

AN URBAN RETREAT PROTECTED BY WALLS, TRELLIS

The photos on this page and the sketch above show a rooftop garden protected on all sides by walls, and overhead by a vine-covered trellis. An exuberant profusion of plants, all in containers, creates a lush oasis in the middle of the city. The plants are complemented by a few carefully selected and placed objects.

In the top photo, an etched glass panel is set into the wall adjacent to a passageway. In the photo at right, a handsome pair of old wrought iron gates guard the entrance to the deck from the passageway. A view of the fountain near the sliding glass doors is shown on page 30. Design: Cole-Wheatman Interior Designers, San Francisco, CA.

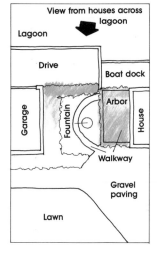

View from houses across lagoon

Lagoon

Drive

Boat dock

Garage

Fountain

Arbor

House

Walkway

Gravel paving

Lawn

A CLASSICAL FOUNTAIN IN A FORMAL BED

In the photo above, a round, classically inspired fountain serves as a center-piece to a symmetrical formal bedding design (sketch at left). Framed by an arbor of honeysuckle and encircled by a dark green hedge of English laurel, the fountain also provides a focus to the view from this wing of the Tiburon, CA house.

A LITTLE SOMETHING FOR THE BIRDS

The strong vertical empha-sis of the bird feeder in the photo at right makes it seem right at home in a woodland garden ablaze with fall color. Design: David Benner, New Hope, PA.

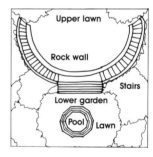

LILY POND DOMINATES A HIDDEN GARDEN

The octagonal lily pond (top photo) is the central feature in a circular garden visible only from the edge of the main garden (see sketch above). Design: Thomas Church, San Francisco, CA.

A STRATEGIC SEAT

The colorful perennial beds of the garden shown at left can be enjoyed to their best advantage from a weathered teak bench. Another view of the same garden is shown on page 6, top.

FUNCTIONAL ORNAMENTS

The ornaments you choose may function in ways other than simply decor, as the photos on this page attest. *Above top:* A pair of iron swans add a note of elegant whimsey to a simply fashioned garden bench. *Above middle:* A small, flowerlike garden light brightens a corner of the garden whether it's on or off. Design: David Poot, Seattle, WA. *Right:* A beautifully aged birdbath is a centerpiece in this restored Colonial garden. Garden of the Heyward-Washington House, The Charleston Museum, Charleston, SC.